Working
in Law
2013

Working in Law 2013

A guide to qualifying and starting a successful legal career

Charlie Phillips

Working in Law 2013: A guide to qualifying and starting a successful legal career

This second edition published in 2012 by Trotman Publishing, a division of Crimson Publishing Ltd, Westminster House, Kew Road, Richmond, Surrey TW9 2ND.

First edition published 2011

© Trotman Publishing 2012

Author: Charlie Phillips

British Library Cataloguing in Publication Data
A catalogue record for this book is available from the British Library.

ISBN 978 1 84455 518 5

Typeset by IDSUK (DataConnection) Ltd
Printed and bound in the UK by Ashford Colour Press, Gosport, Hants

Contents

Contents

Acknowledgements

I would like to thank all the contributors who gave their time to talk about their experiences, and whose insight makes this book a true insiders' view: Fredericka Argent, Ed Chivers, James Evans, David Swain, Daniel Turnbull, Gadi Oron and Katherine Pymont. Thank you also to those I spoke with who preferred to remain anonymous, but whose views and experiences are no less valuable in giving an overview of what to expect when embarking on a career in law.

A special thank you to Walter Bilas and Joanne Rourke for their meticulous review of the text, and comments. Your encouragement and support throughout this project really have been a great help.

Likewise, my thanks are due to Beth Bishop and Jessica Spencer at Trotman for their input and professional guidance, which have been invaluable.

Special thanks to my wife Indre for her support not only during the process of writing this book, but all along my journey to qualification as a solicitor in the first place.

Author's note

A book on law would not be complete without a disclaimer, so: every effort has been made to ensure that this book is accurate and up to date. However, things change, and deadlines, course contents, legal provisions, rules and regulations are likely to change every year. The book is for general guidance only, and readers must check the current state of play, and satisfy themselves of the accuracy of anything set out in the book before taking action. Please note that the text is accompanied by information provided by training institutions, employers and institutions.

Finally, it is impossible to pack every bit of useful information into a book like this, and invariably some things have been left out. The intention was to ensure that what is covered in the book is relevant to the greatest number of people. Additional information, and resources useful to law students and trainees are available on my website (www.charliephillips.info). Suggestions for improvements or additions are welcome!

Charlie Phillips
London, 2012

Introduction

I f you're considering a career in law, then you have already made a good decision. There is a vast range of opportunities available to people with legal qualifications: law is a wide open field, with huge potential for people from all walks of life. In this book we will look in detail at each stage of the qualification process, to help you navigate your way through and decide which areas of law and legal work are best for you. In addition to the facts, you will hear from people who have completed their qualifications, and have gone on to successful legal careers, giving you first-hand insight into what a career in law could really entail.

A career in law can be rewarding, but success will come with overcoming the challenges you'll face along the way. We'll set out what you need to succeed in your chosen discipline – be that as a solicitor, barrister, paralegal or part-qualified lawyer – and how to get there.

In order to get into the legal profession, many people believe that all they need to do is a law degree, another course or two, then perhaps a bit of training. Unfortunately, the truth is slightly more complex than that, and we'll look in detail at the qualifications you'll need in Part 3. It's also not true that you need to have studied a law degree to become a lawyer. There are alternative ways in. Law is, however, a qualification-based profession, so there are several academic and other qualifications you need to get before you can pass from one stage to the next.

A time of diversification

In a period of economic uncertainty, with spending cuts affecting the private and public sectors, it's no surprise that opportunities across the legal profession have become more limited than in previous years. Nevertheless, the number of people looking to a legal career seems to be continually on the increase, leading to many more qualified people than there are jobs for them to take. But even if it looks as though the odds may be stacked against you, remember that there are vacancies out there, and employers are looking for good candidates to fill them. Approach them the right way, and you will succeed.

More people are coming into law from diverse backgrounds than ever before; with many of them offering qualities other than just a set of compulsory academic qualifications. This has led to a genuine increase in diversity across the profession, with more opportunities opening up for people who, in years gone by, may have struggled to get a look in. This means that, contrary to the gloom that the legal profession faced after the recent recession, from another perspective there has never been a better time to get into law, as the profession adjusts to include a more diverse workforce. The increase in applicants has contributed to a view that flexibility within the profession has to be encouraged. For example, it's perfectly acceptable to work as a paralegal or in another part-qualified legal position for a while, before going on to do a training contract or pupillage. In fact, some – perhaps most – employers won't take you seriously without at least some 'hands-on' legal experience.

A broad range of opportunities

There is a wide range of alternative career options available in law, other than the traditional solicitor or barrister routes. These alternatives are open to people with many levels of legal qualification, be that a law degree or conversion degree, or one of the more advanced legal qualifications we will look at later. If you don't manage to get all the way to where you want, there will always be other opportunities that present themselves along the way, to which any legal skills or qualifications will be very well suited. You will find that it's not uncommon to decide that law is generally right for you, but that other professions actually appeal to you more. There is nothing to stop you adjusting your direction as you go, and a legal qualification will always be useful. Were it not for gaining a legal qualification in the first place, you might not have come across these alternatives, and you may not have gained the context in which to come to a firm decision as to which direction to take. We will look at some of the possible career options available to people with legal qualifications in Chapter 12. We've also included a glossary of useful and common terms associated with the world of law, so if you aren't familiar with a term we use in the book, see page 237.

PART 1
Heading into law

1

About working in law

The law covers every aspect of our lives in one way or another, so it's no surprise that working within law presents a wide range of possible career options. You may think the only choice you have to make is between being a solicitor or a barrister, but your options are actually far wider.

The first questions you might be asking yourself are: Why do I want to be a lawyer? Do I have the right academic background to start? Which area of law do I want to work in? We'll look at these, and end this chapter with an overview of the climate of the legal profession today.

Why choose a legal career?

You will probably not be reading this if you are not already at least partially convinced that a career in law is for you. However, it's a good idea to revisit your reasons for making the decision to pursue this career path initially, as these will play a large part in defining where you will end up.

For future solicitors, the pace of life and potentially high salaries of the City may be particularly appealing to some. Others will be looking to work in a particular area, perhaps family law or property, which may offer the opportunity to work as part of the community, rather than part of a commercial enterprise. For barristers, the attraction may be in the independence, responsibility and authority that come with the job, be that at the commercial or criminal bar. With their reputation for intellect, it's perhaps no surprise that there's a good deal of prestige attached to being a barrister.

Here are some of the other main reasons for choosing a career in law.

Intellectual challenge

The strict academic qualifications needed for entry to the profession set the tone for what a lot of the work of a qualified lawyer entails. Wherever you end up, you will need to have a good grasp of the main areas of law, as well as the soft skills that good all-round experience will give you.

All legal practitioners need to keep up their own areas of expertise, but will usually need to draw on a working knowledge of a number of other areas in order to advise their clients effectively. All successful lawyers share a common desire to keep up with developments in law and read around and discuss the subject with colleagues, to absorb and share knowledge just as much as they are required to focus on a particular matter at a particular time.

Barristers versus solicitors

Barristers are known for being experts on technical aspects of law. They are generally called upon to give their expert opinion on the merits of a case, and to assess the strengths and weaknesses, likelihood of success and potential strategy of a case. This can only be done with a very finely tuned expert knowledge of any number of different areas of substantive law, as well as rules governing court procedure, evidence, disclosure and so on – before they even get on their feet to represent their client in court. In addition to knowledge of the various legal areas, effective advocacy requires impeccable verbal presentation, sharp reactions and reasoning skills, knowledge of every last detail of a set of complex facts, and powers of persuasion to reach a successful outcome for the client.

For solicitors, the work is often no less intellectually demanding. A solicitor will very often be required to sift through sets of complex facts to pull out the key areas around which a legal argument can be constructed. Commercial considerations relevant to the matter will also need to be considered. While a barrister's work will usually be in the context of contentious matters that may ultimately reach court, a solicitor working on predominantly non-contentious matters will also deal regularly with detailed technical and factual scenarios.

Salary

You may be enticed into law by the promise of a large salary. Statistics show that salary levels vary greatly within the profession, depending on each lawyer's level of qualification, experience and area of practice. It is true that high salaries are available in some parts of the legal profession, but only a few of the very highly qualified and experienced lawyers earn that much, and it goes without saying that you'll have to work extremely hard over a number of years to get there. Commercial law generally pays better than working in criminal or other state-related sectors of law, as the work relates closely to profit-driven business in one form or another.

Perhaps not surprisingly, the highest salaries are to be found in the commercial City of London law firms and barristers' chambers, with their counterparts in other commercial centres around the country coming a close second. For solicitors, salaries in regional commercial law firms and chambers generally tend to be lower than in London, but will often be at the higher end of the salary range when compared with other professions. 'High-street' firms may focus on a broader range of matters perhaps than the more specialist commercial firms. On a pure salary basis, these firms will pay less than the larger commercial law firms, but will instead offer other incentives – close contact with colleagues and clients, a good deal of responsibility from an early stage, and a sense of contributing to the community.

Making a difference

For many, the attraction of a career in law lies in the possibility of making a positive difference, perhaps to individuals, or to society as a whole. Common to all areas of legal practice are fundamental principles of justice, and in certain areas of legal practice this is particularly prevalent. Criminal law is perhaps the clearest example. Representing a defendant, as either a solicitor or a barrister, will pit the lawyer against the state, in whose name the case has been brought in the interests of wider society. Environmental law is another area where lawyers have a very real opportunity to shape the course of projects with far-reaching implications on the environment, particularly in areas such as mineral exploration, oil and gas. Areas of property law can also have a significant social angle, such as advising large-scale construction projects, or proposing/opposing planning applications. Human rights law, employment and personal injury law are other areas where it is possible for the lawyers' input to have a positive social effect.

Diversity of career options

Legal work offers a wide range of options, both at the start and as you progress and gain legal experience. Wherever you start off working in law, you will always come across new legal issues, areas of law you have less experience with, and which may present opportunities for you as your career develops.

Your contribution counts

Regardless of your level of qualification, it is very rewarding to see your work being used and valued, perhaps in its own right or as part of a broader matter. A high level of productivity will be required from you in any area of law you work in, and very seldom will you be expected to be an observer. Feeding into this productivity gives you the opportunity to make your mark, and see your contribution count.

Career resilience and employability

Any legal qualification helps put you ahead of your non-qualified peers. Competition for qualified roles is tough, and we will look at this in more detail later, but legal qualifications are viewed positively because they are relevant to many employers. This is very helpful as you apply for any role, either now or in the future. Legal qualifications and experience can be portable from one area of work to another, which can be a great advantage when approaching the job market.

Dynamic working environment

Any legal matter may change and take an unexpected direction as it progresses, requiring agility and the ability to react and adapt strategy accordingly. This makes for an interesting and vibrant working environment. When this is added to the changing backdrops of updated legislation and new case law, and the challenges posed in reacting to or working around these developments, it is easy to see why many people are attracted to the dynamic nature of legal work.

International angle

There is an international angle to most, if not all, legal matters. UK legislation in all areas is shaped by developments in Europe, while cross-border trade plays an increasingly important role in the global economy. Whether you decide to specialise in international law or not, it is likely you will come across international issues in many areas of legal work.

Status and perceived value

Obtaining any legal qualification requires dedication, hard work and a certain amount of intellect. As such, there is some kudos and status attached to them. There is much more to this than vanity, however. From a professional perspective, the positive perception of legal qualifications can be very useful, as there is a common understanding of one's level of knowledge or experience, which is easily communicated. This helps in the workplace and boosts employability.

The qualities you need for law

Handling responsibility

You can expect to be given a good deal of responsibility from the start of your legal career, and the rewards and accountability that come with it. An introduction to the kinds of responsibility you might expect as a lawyer may come during some of the assessments during the Academic and Vocational stages of training (see Chapters 6 and 7). Written exams and other assessments, such as mock client interviews or applications to court, are a good indicator of the level of personal responsibility you will take as your career progresses: you will often be expected to prepare and present aspects of a matter on your own, and while you will usually receive a good level of support, the ability to handle work autonomously is an essential skill.

Willingness to learn

Good research, reasoning and written skills are essential for any lawyer, as are good verbal presentation, personal organisation, self-motivation and persistence. There is a steep learning curve at the start of any legal career, and you never stop learning as your career progresses. It is important to develop the ability to take criticism well, and treat this as an essential part of the process. Most legal roles will provide training and development that will seek to enhance these 'soft' skills, in addition to developing more technical legal skills.

Intellectual ability

In order to gain the qualifications needed to go from one stage of training to the next, all lawyers need a good level of academic and intellectual ability. It is not enough simply to have passed the exams, however. Legal work can be complex and challenging, and it is essential to have an interest in keeping up with the more 'academic' aspects of the law, as well as the more practical ones.

Capacity for hard work

You won't be slaving away in the office until 3a.m. every day, but you will be expected to work hard. Be realistic about this from the outset: the academic qualifications require a lot of effort, so does the professional training, and that's before you qualify. On qualification, a new set of factors come into play, requiring a new set of skills that takes time to develop. It doesn't always come easily, so be prepared to work hard, as that's the way to get ahead.

Working with people

Perhaps the most important aspect of a lawyer's work is the ability to work with people, and the importance of good communication cannot be over-emphasised. You need to develop professional relationships with a wide range of people at all levels and be able to get on with people, understanding differing viewpoints and levels of experience.

Commercial awareness

Most legal work contains a commercial or financial element, and the majority of commercial legal work focuses exclusively on this. It is therefore essential to have a good sense of commercial awareness (which we look at more on page 135). You also need to understand the value of offering a good service to your clients, and be keen to get some satisfaction out of offering excellent service.

Integrity

The legal system is, at its most fundamental level, intended to serve the interests of society, and lawyers have a duty to further this interest. Professional conduct across the profession is set out in a number of rules, and it is essential to understand these obligations. Different areas of law face different ethical or professional challenges, and a good sense of integrity goes a long way to approaching potential issues in the most appropriate way. You'll be placed in positions of trust as well as responsibility, which can require skills that can't be learned from textbooks.

Common sense and self-awareness

It may sound obvious, but an essential requirement for all lawyers is common sense. Throughout your career you will be faced with situations where you may not immediately have a clear idea of what you should do, or what the most suitable option is to take. Very often, however, using your common sense is all you need to get yourself through a seemingly difficult situation. The same approach applies to studying, making job applications, interviews, or when tackling any other aspect of the qualification process. You are often being assessed on how you approach an issue, rather than on your technical legal skills.

An overview of the academic requirements needed

Now we've looked at some of the reasons you might want to work in law, and the personal attributes you need, we'll look at the fundamental academic requirements that are essential when embarking on a legal career.

Regardless of which route you decide to take in law, the starting points are very similar. There are a number of entry requirements for each of the academic qualifications, which must all be completed successfully before candidates can continue to the next level. It's worth mentioning this right at the start for a couple of reasons.

- These are strict requirements. While it's sometimes possible to start a qualifying law degree or equivalent conversion course without A levels, the remaining academic and vocational steps are compulsory requirements for full qualification.

- In order to get a training position within a solicitors' firm or barristers' chambers, you will need a law degree or conversion, and the relevant vocational qualifications: either the Legal Practice Course (LPC) for solicitors, or the Bar Professional Training Course (BPTC; formerly the Bar Vocational Course) for barristers.

Sticklers for results

The fact that all this academic training is required should give an indication of the nature of the work you'll be doing once you are working in law. When assessing new recruits, lawyers, who tend to be naturally risk averse, will view academic achievements as a fairly reliable way of benchmarking the extent to which a candidate is likely to be a successful fit into their team. The higher the academic achievements, the lower the potential risk of taking on that candidate. There will always be exceptions to this, but it gives employers a starting point, and it's one that applies to everyone.

The stages of qualification

The main stages of qualification for solicitors and barristers can be broken down into five main areas.

1. Your previously existing academic qualifications (GCSEs, A levels, etc.).

2. The 'Academic Stage' for all lawyers.

3. The 'Vocational Stage' for solicitors and barristers.

4. Professional training (training contract or pupillage).

5. Post-qualification requirements.

	Stage 1		Stage 2	Stage 3	
A levels, GCSEs or equivalent	'Academic Stage' of training		'Vocational Stage' of training	Professional training	Post-qualification
	Law degree or conversion degree: Graduate Diploma in Law (GDL) (if non-law degree)	Solicitors*:	Legal Practice Course (LPC)	Training contract	Continuing professional development
		Barristers:	Bar Professional Training Course (BPTC)	Pupillage	Continuing professional development

* Legal executives: the Chartered Institute of Legal Executives (CILEx) route is also available to gain equivalent qualifications to each of stages 1–3 (see below).

Stage 1: The 'Academic Stage'

Undergraduate-level law degree, or equivalent conversion degree

Law degree courses

If your first degree is in law from a recognised course provider, then great: you will now have what is referred to as a 'qualifying law degree'. You will have had three years working through the various legal subjects, and you can now progress directly to the Vocational Stage of qualification, via the Legal Practice Course (LPC) or Bar Professional Training Course (BPTC) (see below).

Note that some course providers now offer qualifying law degrees that span two years, instead of the traditional three.

Law conversion degrees

If you have a degree in a subject other than law, you will need to complete the Graduate Diploma in Law (GDL), or less commonly the Common Professional Examination (CPE), which are both often referred to as a 'conversion degree'. These courses compress the key contents of a three-year law degree into one academic year (or two years part-time).

A conversion degree is a convenient way of getting onto the legal ladder. There are advantages and disadvantages to both the conversion degree and the qualifying law degree routes, but, in practice, it doesn't matter which you take. As long as you have a relatively solid understanding of the course material (and some good grades!) then you'll be fine. You're at the start of a long journey, so in just the same way that no one expects you to be an expert driver just after passing your driving test, neither will anyone expect you to be an authority on any aspect of law before you have even started the Vocational Stage – not at this stage, at least.

The Academic Stage qualifications are looked at in more detail in Chapter 6.

Stage 2: The 'Vocational Stage'

Vocational courses for solicitors and barristers

Once you have your qualifying law degree or conversion qualification, the next step of the academic process is to complete a vocational course. These courses are different for solicitors and barristers, and it is at this stage that their routes to qualification split: you have to decide on one or the other. We discuss the difference between training and working as a solicitor and barrister in depth in Chapter 5, if you haven't already made up your mind on which route to pursue.

Solicitors' Vocational Stage of training

The Solicitors' Legal Practise Course (LPC) builds on the main theoretical legal areas covered on a law degree, and sets them in a more practical context. The LPC is split into compulsory areas and optional areas. It is at the stage of choosing these options (known as 'electives') that you will effectively start to specialise, as you will need to make some decisions to narrow the course options to fit the areas of legal practice that you are most interested in.

Barristers' Vocational Stage of training

Barristers will need to complete the Bar Professional Training Course (BPTC). The objective of the BPTC is similar to that of the LPC, in that it equips students with the skills necessary for practice as a barrister, by building on the knowledge acquired during the Academic Stage of training. There are compulsory and optional elements to the BPTC, with the emphasis being on case preparation, giving advice on cases and claims, and advocacy (representing clients in courts and tribunals).

The Vocational Stage qualifications are looked at in more detail in Chapter 7.

Stage 3: Professional training

With your Academic and Vocational stages done, the next step to qualification is either the solicitors' training contract or barristers' pupillage. These are similar to apprenticeships, as the trainee or pupil gains essential hands-on experience by assisting qualified lawyers over the course of several months, learning to apply the theoretical knowledge gained so far in the context of real-life legal practice. There's more on this in Chapter 10.

Solicitors' professional training

The solicitors' training contract generally takes two years. Trainee solicitors will usually be employed by a solicitors' firm on a fixed-term contract, and will be exposed to a range of work by assisting qualified solicitors in different departments. The time spent in each department is known as a 'seat'.

In addition to the practical work, all trainees must pass a Professional Skills Course (PSC). This ensures that all solicitors receive training in important aspects of legal practice such as money laundering and the ethical aspects of a solicitor's work. The PSC involves a couple of written tests, and some role-play type assessments, but is not nearly as intensive as the GDL or LPC. A couple of alternative routes to qualification exist, such as that offered by the Chartered Institute of Legal Executives (CILEx). Again, we'll look at these in more detail in Chapter 7.

Barristers' professional training

Once a future barrister has passed the BPTC, they will need to complete a 'pupillage' in order to become fully qualified. A pupillage usually takes one year, and is divided into two six-month periods, spent assisting a junior barrister with five or more years of experience. The first six months are usually spent in a non-practising capacity, shadowing and assisting the pupil supervisor. The second six months involve the pupil playing a much more active role, continuing to assist the supervisor, but also running matters of their own, with appropriate supervision. After successfully completing pupillage, a barrister is fully qualified, and entitled to set up his or her own practice, taking a room in a set of barristers' chambers (known as taking a 'tenancy').

We will look at all this in a lot more detail in Part 3, so don't worry if it sounds complex. The main point at this stage is to understand that there are a number of academic hurdles to get over. Making sure you have a realistic chance of getting through these – and that you have the time and the stamina required – is very important.

Research for the future

When it comes to applying for professional training positions, your credibility as an applicant will increase dramatically the more real-life legal experience you have, so get out there and find some! It's essential to start forming your own view of what the legal profession is all about, and how you may fit into it.

At this early stage of your career search, the main aim is to learn the landscape of the profession, how solicitors and barristers work, how the support roles work, and what happens day to day in the life of someone already in the position you one day hope to reach yourself.

- Research areas you're interested in and read as much as you can on the subject (this book is a good start).

- Speak to your college or university law tutors and careers advisers.

- Look around for any contacts in law you have already, and ask whether you can do a work placement or shadow them.

- Familiarise yourself with the official regulators and bodies, as you will deal with them throughout your career (see page 245).

Career progression

Which specific areas of law appeal to you, and what do you know about the careers and positions that relate to those areas? You may be thinking that there are only two paths to choose from – solicitor or barrister – but in reality there is a wide range of options available for both, in private practice (in a law firm for solicitors, or in chambers for barristers) or working in-house for a non-legal organisation.

There are fairly well-defined career paths available in most areas of legal practice, allowing you a certain level of control over where your future may lie. Of course, there are no guarantees, but you are more likely to know what your long-term prospects as a lawyer might be than in other, less qualification-driven walks of life. Below we look at how your qualifications and career progression could work out.

Solicitors in private practice law firms

For solicitors, each full year following qualification counts towards an overall tally of post-qualification experience or PQE. For the first year following qualification, solicitors are referred to as 'newly qualifieds' or NQs. Within law firms, less-experienced solicitors of up to around five years' PQE are often referred to as 'associates' or 'assistants', as well as just 'solicitors'. With a few more years' PQE, they may become 'senior associates', at which point they will usually be looking at being made a partner. Partnership is generally as high as it gets within many law firms. Partners share overall responsibility for the performance of the firm, which means taking a share of the profits (and taking home more than salaried staff), but also sharing the liability for the firm's performance. This may mean taking the occasional pay cut during tough times, or being ultimately responsible for anything done in error or negligence within the firm, subject to the firm's insurance cover.

Barristers

Practising barristers working from chambers are self-employed from qualification all the way through their career. In essence, these barristers fall into two categories according to experience: 'junior' or Queen's Counsel (QC). A junior may have many years of qualification (or 'call'), and an experienced junior barrister can be referred to as a 'senior junior'. QCs are barristers who have been selected on the basis of exceptional ability, and represent the most senior level of the profession. QCs are often selected as judges, and it is also possible for QCs to sit as judges at the same time as continuing their barristers' practice.

In-house lawyers

For many solicitors and barristers, life in a firm or practising at the Bar is not as appealing as working in-house. Every organisation, in every sector, is faced with a range of legal issues every day. These may include employment law issues with staff, property questions with leases or ownership of premises, or commercial contract points, and may perhaps lead to litigation if there is a dispute. Depending on the nature of the organisation, there will often be a range of regulatory rules to consider, governing everything from health and safety to local council rules. In-house lawyers deal with all the day-to-day legal issues that their organisation faces, and the variety of this kind of work can be very rewarding. Of course, it's impossible for any one lawyer – or even a team of in-house lawyers – to be experts in every field, so the expertise of external lawyers is often drawn upon for more specialist or business-critical matters. In-house lawyers tend to enjoy the detailed knowledge of the business that they gain from effectively having only one client, and can become leaders in their field. They can also become specialist legal advisers in their own right.

Part-qualified lawyers: legal executives and paralegals

Legal executives usually work in a particular area of law, and their work is similar to that of a junior solicitor. CILEx offers a set of qualifications for legal executives (see Chapter 7). One of the principal remits of CILEx is to offer its members flexible legal training and professional development. CILEx helps its members achieve the full range of qualifications required for each level of the profession, from diploma and A level, to part qualification as legal secretaries or paralegals, all the way up to fully qualified status.

Paralegals often assist solicitors with fee-earning work, but are not trainees or qualified solicitors. There is no formal level of qualification required to become a paralegal, and the Law Society does not directly regulate their activities, so there can be a great deal of flexibility to a paralegal role. Many view paralegal work as an opportunity to gain valuable hands-on legal work experience, working in a firm with the ultimate objective of gaining a training contract, and to progress from there on to qualification. Others are career paralegals, who have amassed a huge amount of experience in a particular area of law, and make their paralegal work an end in itself.

In Part 3 we will look at the process of getting qualified, from making the early decisions right up to what happens at qualification and beyond. There's no doubting that it can be tricky at times, but the rewards are well worth the effort you put in. The key to success lies in assessing your options realistically at the outset, and we will help you do exactly that.

Do I need previous work experience?

In more specialist areas of law, previous experience is a definite advantage. The fact that the GDL allows a law degree to be fit into one year makes it relatively quick for those wishing to qualify with experience in other areas to do so. Previous working experience in the area of law in which you wish to practise will put you in very good stead. There are numerous examples of specialist lawyers working in all manner of areas who came to law from previous careers, in areas such as financial regulation, the media, information technology (IT), and many others. Of course, some organisations offer the opportunity to train in-house and to qualify internally. While not strictly necessary, previous legal work experience will count very favourably, and will help both employer and employee get the most out of the investment in training and qualification.

The competitive climate

The law is a competitive and specialist profession. Standards are high, as are the potential rewards, but so is demand for the opportunities available. There are more people than ever coming into law, with more applicants applying for the same places on courses, and going on to apply for the same training contract or pupillage positions. Your challenge is to be the best of the bunch, and you should have this firmly in mind from the outset.

Solicitors are on the increase

The number of newly qualified solicitors is still increasing, despite economic pressures: 3.5% more qualified solicitors were registered in December 2011 than at the same time in 2010. While this increase demonstrates that more people are progressing through the various stages of training to ultimately gain full qualification, the availability of jobs for them to take has not necessarily increased at a matching rate. The long-term effects of this are hard to assess, but it is possible that increased competition will reduce job opportunities within the profession.

Solicitors passing the professional stage

Each year, more than 14,000 full- and part-time LPC places are available, with an average of over 9,000 students passing the LPC. In 2010, the LPC pass rate was 89.7%. Assuming you have the required grades for entry, you shouldn't have any problems getting a place.[1]

In 2010, 4,784 training contracts were registered with the Law Society, down approximately 1,000 on the previous year.[2] As a very rough average, there were therefore only enough training positions available in England and Wales for 54% of the people who passed the LPC.

According to the *AGR Graduate Recruitment Summer Survey 2011*, there were on average 65.5 applications for every training contract position.

Retention rates for solicitors

Be very careful when you look at published or quoted retention rates of trainees at law firms, particularly the larger ones. It doesn't look good when a firm does not retain the very people they have invested time and money in training up. If trainees are not kept on, awkward questions are asked: Is the firm doing badly? Are they taking on the wrong people at trainee level? Is their training policy flawed? The result is that firms will tend to put a positive spin on their trainee retention figures, regardless of the real situation. 'Trainee retention' does not mean 'trainees who were given qualified solicitors' roles immediately on qualification'. A firm may give qualified roles to only three out of six trainees, and may offer paralegal or business development roles to the others. In this example, the fact that job offers were made to all trainees means the firm can say they had 100% retention, when in reality only 50% were offered fully qualified roles. Nevertheless, an offer of a part-qualified role means the firm doesn't want to lose you, and your role might develop into a fully qualified role over time.

Barrister positions remain competitive

The situation for prospective barristers has always been tough, and their profession has not seen the same increases in numbers reaching qualification in recent years as for solicitors. As has long been the case, the likelihood of an applicant to the BPTC going all the way to securing tenancy remains low. As a general guide, the Bar Council states that the BPTC is completed by approximately 1,700 students each year, while the number of pupillage places available across the country recently dipped to below 500. Even when pupillage is secured, not all barristers go on to secure tenancy.

While this may sound gloomy, remember that there *are* pupillage positions out there, and with the right approach and commitment, suitably qualified candidates are very much in demand.

Professional stage (barristers)

Entry requirements are relatively strict. There are approximately 3,000 applications for 1,800 places on the BPTC, and the Bar Council's Bar Standards Board is planning on introducing both an aptitude test and an English language test for BPTC applicants whose first language is not English or Welsh. See Chapter 7 for more details on the aptitude test.

Most years, fewer than 500 newly qualified barristers take up tenancy after pupillage, while just over 200 take up jobs as employed barristers. The success rate of BPTC applicants ultimately continuing to pupillage and then taking up tenancy is only 17%. Adding employed barristers into the equation, the figures look slightly better, at approximately 24%.

Given the investment in time and money required just to get through the BPTC, do think about the success rates for barristers, and plan your future accordingly. The statistics alone should not put you off, but keep in mind alternative career options along the way (see Chapter 12).

Profile: The Law Society of England and Wales

The Law Society

Becoming a solicitor

Solicitors combine legal expertise and people skills to provide expert confidential legal advice and assistance, in direct contact with clients.

Becoming a solicitor can be competitive and expensive. Those willing to invest time and effort will enter a career that can be incredibly rewarding, but the qualification process requires academic and financial commitment and will take at least five years. Approximately 8,000 individuals qualify each year.

If you are interested in becoming a solicitor you should do your research. Talk to people in the profession and seek some work experience. This will help you to decide whether you and the profession are right for each other, as well as demonstrating to recruiters that you are serious about a career in law.

A wide range of career options

Solicitors have a variety of career options: in private practice; within a business or organisation; in local or central government; or in court services.

Routes into the profession

There are three main routes to qualifying as a solicitor.

1. The law graduate route

The majority of solicitors qualify by this route. The key stages are:

- qualifying law degree – three years
- Legal Practice Course – one year
- training contract – two years.

A 'qualifying' law degree meets the requirements of the Solicitors Regulation Authority and the Bar Standards Board and is valid for entry to the Legal Practice Course for up to seven years after graduation.

2. The non-law graduate route

Approximately 20% of solicitors qualify by this route. The key stages are:

- degree in any subject – three years
- Common Professional Examination/Graduate Diploma in Law – one year (for non-law graduates)
- Legal Practice Course – one year
- training contract – two years.

Find out more on the above routes to qualification at the Solicitors Regulation Authority website, www.sra.org.uk, and the Law Society careers website at www.lawsociety.org.uk/careersinlaw/becomingasolicitor.page.

3. The Chartered Institute of Legal Executives (CILEx) routes

Qualification through CILEx routes takes longer than by other routes and is designed to enable individuals to study while working. As a CILEx fellow you may work as a legal executive, or you may go on to qualify as a solicitor. In some circumstances you may be exempted from the training contract. Find out more at www.cilex.org.uk.

Training contract

After Academic and Vocational stages comes practice-based training, or a 'training contract'. Stiff competition means training contract applications are usually made during the second year of university. Trainees apply, under supervision, the skills and knowledge acquired during their Academic and Vocational stages. Most training contracts are in private practice, but also are offered within local and central government, commerce and industry, Crown Prosecution Service, Her Magesty's Courts and Tribunals Service and other organisations. Details of employers authorised to take on trainee solicitors can be found at www. lawsociety.org.uk under 'Find a solicitor'.

Support for junior lawyers

The Junior Law Division (JLD) of the Law Society represents all student members of the Law Society enrolled through the Solicitors Regulation Authority, trainees, and solicitors with up to five years' active experience. It provides its members with support, advice, information and networking opportunities and provides a voice for students and trainees through lobbying and campaigns. A mentoring scheme matches members to more experienced fellow solicitors for advice and support on work-related issues. Student members can enrol through the Solicitors Regulation Authority while trainee solicitors are enrolled automatically.

Preparing students for gaining entry to the solicitors' profession

A free careers event for undergraduates is held biannually, covering all aspects of preparation for a career in the solicitors' profession and including tips on gaining relevant experience, completing applications and interview techniques. The range of career options is also represented by the many employers who participate.

Diversity Access Scheme

The Law Society Diversity Access Scheme aims to improve social mobility in the legal profession by supporting promising entrants who face significant social, educational, financial or personal obstacles to qualification, for example homelessness, time in local authority care, overcoming coercion into arranged marriage or severe physical disabilities. All have shown tenacity, courage and commitment in the pursuit of their career. The Diversity Access Scheme has helped 101 students to date.

Changes in legal education and training

Three legal regulators, the Solicitors Regulation Authority, Bar Standards Board and CILEx Professional Services, are currently reviewing legal education and training in England and Wales. An independent research team is expected to make recommendations by December 2012.

Visit www.letr.org.uk for more information, or to stay up to date with the progress of the review. You can also send any comments to the Law Society, at educationandtraining@lawsociety.org.uk.

Case study

A BPTC student yet to secure pupillage warns of the need to be informed from the outset

It pays to be realistic before starting out, because entering the legal profession is a costly business! In order to become a barrister you have no choice but to complete the BPTC, but it is recommended that you do not consider it unless you have pupillage secured.

This makes sense for two reasons: first, there is a chance (albeit a small one) that the chambers will reimburse you, at least in part, for your BPTC fees; and second, the training you have had is fresh in your mind, which may give you some confidence when starting pupillage.

Since September 2010, anyone graduating from Bar school no longer has the right to call themselves a 'non-practising barrister' – they can only give themselves the barrister title if they complete pupillage. This means that if you are a student who does not have pupillage, you are paying £15,000 to attend Bar school with no employment or title at the end of it.

THE LAW SOCIETY of SCOTLAND
www.lawscot.org.uk

Supporting new lawyers

Considering or currently studying law?

The Law Society of Scotland provides comprehensive information and advice to help tomorrow's lawyers make informed decisions for their future.

Contact us at newlawyers@lawscot.org.uk or visit **www.lawscot.org.uk/becomingasolicitor** to find out more.

Profile: The Law Society of Scotland

Heather McKendrick, Development Officer, Education and Training, at the Law Society of Scotland discusses the route to qualification

Being a Scottish qualified solicitor is held in high regard throughout the business world and by solicitors from other countries. The standard of education and professionalism which solicitors must attain, and which continues throughout the working life of a solicitor, means that it is recognised as a highly respected profession which can lead to a varied career, whichever career path is chosen.

Scots law (the LLB) can be studied as a first degree in 10 higher education institutions in Scotland. This can take two, three or, more commonly, four years. The single honours law degree, which is taken by the majority of students, takes four years. The ordinary degree takes three, and the accelerated ordinary degree, for those with a first degree in another discipline, takes two. It is also possible to study law as a joint honours degree at several institutions.

For those who do not wish to obtain an LLB degree, an alternative route to qualification exists. This involves entering into a three-year pre-diploma training contract with a Scottish solicitor and studying for the Society's professional exams. It should be noted that people who take this alternative route are still required to obtain a Diploma in Professional Legal Practice and to undertake a two-year post-diploma traineeship. This route has been reviewed in recent years and there is a commitment to retain it until a replacement can be found. However, it is likely that within the next few years the emphasis of the pre-diploma training contract will change significantly to reflect changes elsewhere on the route to qualification. It is likely that these changes will be coupled with other flexible options for entrance to the solicitors' profession.

For the vast majority of people in Scotland the route to qualification as a solicitor comprises three stages: the LLB, followed by the Diploma in Professional Legal Practice and finally the traineeship. Upon completion of the first stage, the LLB, students wishing to qualify as a solicitor in Scotland undertake the Diploma in Professional Legal Practice, also known as PEAT 1 (Professional Education and Training Stage 1). This is the postgraduate Vocational Stage which has been developed to teach the practical knowledge and skills necessary for the working life of a solicitor. Currently it is possible to undertake the diploma at six universities in Scotland. Up to 50% of the content of PEAT 1 can be elective, meaning that students have a real choice regarding the areas of law they might later wish to practise in.

The final stage in the route to qualification is PEAT 2 – Professional Education and Training Stage 2 which is the two-year work-based or in-office stage and shares the outcomes of PEAT 1. This is where the knowledge, skills, attitudes and values taught in PEAT 1 are honed in the working environment. During PEAT 2, trainees need to undertake 60 hours of trainee continuing professional development (TCPD) and will work towards meeting the standard of the 'qualifying solicitor.'

To ensure strong links between the Vocational and work-based stage, the Society has introduced common outcomes which span both stages. This means that those graduating from PEAT 1 all meet a defined minimum standard that training firms can rely upon.

The Law Society of Scotland is here to support solicitors throughout their career, from giving information to school leavers about careers in law, to giving professional guidance and support.

Heather McKendrick, Development Officer, Education and Training, the Law Society of Scotland.

Case study

Arezo Darvishzadeh is a trainee solicitor at HBJ Gateley LLP. She describes her career and life as a trainee solicitor

I was always attracted to entering a profession that would be challenging and diverse whilst enabling me to use my problem-solving and research skills; for me, law encompasses all of this. Law is constantly evolving and updating, which means even after I have left university, I am still learning on a daily basis.

The route to qualification as a solicitor is not easy. The application and interview process is particularly tough in the current economic climate. It is important for prospective trainees to make themselves stand out and this can be achieved either academically and/or through skills gained from non-academic experiences. My advice would be to try and create a well-rounded CV through both work experience and extra-curricular activities as it should make interview and application questions easier to answer!

Attending law fairs can be very helpful in terms of getting an idea of what employers are looking for as well as getting a better idea of the differences between organisations, law firms and practice areas. In terms of gaining a traineeship, there is a range of options available, including commercial or criminal; small, medium or large law firms; and public sector, private sector or in-house traineeships. The structure of the traineeship can also vary from multiple 'seats' lasting a number of months each, to a single seat in one practice area or indeed a general traineeship with no particular practice area assigned.

I am currently in the second of my four six-month seats, working within the Corporate Department in the Edinburgh office of HBJ Gateley. Typically my workload includes drafting and completing Companies House forms, compiling bibles, preparing ancillary documents (e.g. board minutes, resolutions, certificates, etc.) and conducting research. On an average day, I arrive at my desk for 8.30a.m. and leave around 6p.m.

My first seat was a shared litigation and construction seat, and this included some time working in our Glasgow office. In contrast to the Corporate Department, I was mainly involved in contentious work and my workload included appearing in court, drafting letters of advice, lodging motions and defences, attending court with fee earners to take notes, conducting research and court running.

During my time at the firm, I have had the opportunity to attend various events organised by the firm including the Firm Handshake event (a networking event for young professionals) and Sportsquest (a large charity event organised and sponsored by HBJ Gateley), enabling me to observe business development from an early stage in my career. The firm also places a great deal of emphasis on corporate social responsibility, with a focus on charity, community, people and environmental projects. Through this, I have attended the Transition into Work day, which involved me speaking to groups of primary school students about the realities of working in the legal profession.

2

What working in law is really like

Popular myths about working in law

Legal qualifications have meaning and value because they are subject to carefully regulated standards. The academic courses and exams are not easy, and the Vocational and professional stages of training are also taxing. Competition is tough – for training contracts and pupillages in particular – so it is inevitable that a number of myths have sprung up about working in law, which aren't all that helpful. Here are some of the more popular myths, and how they measure up to reality.

'Everyone doing law has 15 A* at GCSE and 5 A* at A level'

You will find that the majority of applicants don't have such illustrious credentials. You will inevitably need to have solid, consistent grades, but a full house of nothing but the very highest scores may suggest you're only good on paper, and that you've spent your life holed up, studying alone. You need to have some extra-curricular and commercial experience on hand, to show a more balanced skill set. You'll need good grades, but grades alone don't tell an employer anything about your personality and people skills, which are essential elements for any lawyer.

'Everybody in law went to Oxford or Cambridge'

There are far more people working in law than there are Oxbridge graduates, so this clearly isn't true. While it's important to get consistently good grades, it's also vital to get a 2.i to get a look in at most firms and chambers. A 2.i from a lesser-known university is still a 2.i, and it will be up to you to demonstrate in applications and interviews how much you applied yourself, and how much you got out of your time, wherever you studied. An Oxbridge graduate with a 2.ii still has a 2.ii. They will find it much harder to progress in law without a well thought-out strategy, not least because the majority of online application forms simply won't let you progress unless you can tick the '2.i' box. It can be done, but it's a lot harder.

Regardless of where you studied at undergraduate level, you must focus on getting the best grades you can, particularly on your law conversion, LPC or BPTC. Your legal grades can be viewed as far more relevant than where you happen to have studied at undergraduate level.

'There are so few training contracts to go round that it's hardly worth applying'

It's true that there are not many training contracts or pupillages available, and far fewer than there are applicants to fill them. Nevertheless, the positions do exist, and are waiting to be filled by people with the right skills and qualifications. It's not easy, but with the right strategy you can hugely increase your chances of putting in good applications, getting interviews and ultimately securing that elusive place. In Chapter 11 we will concentrate on strategy and tactics that will help you get a training contract or pupillage, and in Chapter 13 we will look at the alternative routes to qualification that are available for those for whom the traditional route is not working out, or for whom it just isn't appropriate.

'Day-to-day work in law is a nightmare, with very long hours, late nights and weekends all thrown in'

You will be expected to work as long and as hard as anyone else; indeed, at junior level you may be required to work longer and harder than your more qualified colleagues. You have the disadvantages of lack of experience, legal knowledge and context, and early on in your career you may not even know where things are in the office, or who the right person is to ask when you're not sure of something. All this adds to a challenging working environment. Occasionally you may have to stay late, and it has been known that some overnight and weekend work can be involved. One thing always holds true, however – no one likes working late, including supervisors. If the work is urgent or important enough to justify long or out-of-hours work, then this is an opportunity to demonstrate commitment. Make sure you get the context and background to the work from supervisors or colleagues. You'll learn more from the experience and you'll be more useful. Moreover, you can take a lot of positive value from what might otherwise have not been such a positive experience.

'As a junior lawyer, you only do menial work, such as photocopying'

All legal work is varied, even at junior level, but you have to start somewhere. Having said that, there are great variances in what is expected at the very start. For barristers, the nature of their work means they are expected to hit the ground running, perhaps more than for trainee solicitors. Trainee solicitors may well start off by being given work that probably doesn't need to be done by someone on their way to a high-level legal qualification. However, there are good reasons for being given menial work, at least initially. Usually, it is simply because something is needed urgently, and you are there to do it.

A supervisor should be able to count on the reliability, attention to detail and overall competence that a trainee solicitor can offer, to ensure that whatever they are given will be done well and on time. Some firms start trainees off low, to test their aptitude (and attitude!). The better you do, the more likely you are to get better quality work that is more appropriate to your level of ability. Lawyers are naturally cautious. They are not going to set you, as a newly arrived trainee, on the most important client matter they are working on, until they know with a good degree of certainty what your skills and abilities are, and that they can rely on you. It's up to you to fast track your way to this level of responsibility. This can be done, and often a lot quicker than you may think.

'You're only a real lawyer if you work in a firm or chambers. In-house doesn't count'

A perception may exist that in-house legal positions have less appeal than positions in a specialist legal practice. However, you only have to look at the roles and responsibilities of senior lawyers at some of the country's biggest companies to know that this is of course a myth.

Solicitors in private practice, and barristers in chambers, are legal specialists, but very often in-house counsel have superior knowledge of their sector than many private practice lawyers. Day-to-day contact with their sector can give in-house lawyers the edge on legal and commercial issues affecting their business.

'It's worth paying for all the course fees, because you make a killing when you qualify'

The salaries on offer in law vary greatly depending on which route you take, and are not always as high as you might expect, given the level of qualification needed. Your legal courses will always cost money, and there is no guarantee of success at the end. However, every qualification you gain puts you a step ahead, so the sensible thing is to plan each stage of your qualification carefully. Don't stretch yourself on the assumption that things might work out in the end. Instead, make sure you can justify each course, and each week of work experience, or time spent in junior-level roles that you may get along the way to build your CV.

Of course, you may need to take out a loan, or otherwise subsidise your course fees (we will talk about that in more detail later on), but the important thing is to ensure that you get something positive for yourself out of each stage of your training, without needing to rely on specific job offers, or input from third parties.

The truth about salaries

The attraction of high salaries may draw a lot of people to law, but the reality can be very different. Salaries vary greatly depending on what type of work you do, what type of firm or organisation you work for, and where in the country you work. You should do as much research as you can in the areas you are most interested in, to get the most accurate information on what the salaries might be, and to make sure your expectations are realistic.

Be aware that the law evolves, and with this comes the risk that some areas of law become less widely applicable over time, less commercially viable, and therefore less profitable. The law is not immune to outside pressures and was affected just as badly by the 2008/09 recession as any other service industry. Many law firms were forced to consolidate their operations, and in many cases had to make redundancies.

A City solicitor tells you what you need to know about salaries

'Don't expect an easy ride: people see the big salaries, but that isn't always the case, particularly as you make your way up the ladder. The glamorous image that people have through watching Suits, LA Law or Ally McBeal just isn't the case.

'As you work your way through law, legislation is constantly changing, which means that areas of the law that might have been lucrative in the past may no longer be. You never know the changes that may come along as the law changes. For example, the Jackson Review on civil litigation costs was published in December 2009, with implications as to how cases be funded, especially "no win, no fee" arrangements.

'Similarly, the introduction of licensed conveyancers has changed the property law/conveyancing market. You no longer have to pay qualified solicitors' rates to get conveyancing work done, which has reduced the value of this kind of work. And when a recession hits, the legal market can be badly affected. I know of *several firms where entire departments were made redundant. It's getting better now, but you have to bear in mind that even full qualification is no guarantee of a job for life.'*

Trainee solicitors

Until September 2011, the Law Society set a minimum salary for trainees. For trainees working in London this was £18,590, and for those working outside London it was £16,650. However, following a consultation on the minimum salary system, the Solicitors Regulation Authority announced in May 2012 that no minimum salary would be obligatory for trainees from August 2014 onwards. The only obligation for employers would be to pay the national minimum wage. Many commercial firms pay their trainees at a competitive rate, though; some firms (inside and outside London) pay around £25,000, and some of the larger City firms pay in excess of £35,000.

Again, do your research. Many firms publish their trainee salaries on their websites, as part of their strategy to recruit the best applicants. If it is difficult to find out how much you are likely to be paid, then it is reasonable to ask a firm what the expected or current salary ranges are. You may not feel comfortable asking about this in an interview, but there should be an opportunity to ask human resources (HR) or another representative along the application process. This could be done either when making initial enquiries, or perhaps when following up on an application. If a firm is reluctant to give you an indication of salaries in writing (including by email), then you may have more luck making a phone call and asking for a 'ball park' estimate, on the understanding that this is just to help you get an idea of what to expect.

Paid to take a year out?

There was a lot of press activity in 2009 and 2010, when trainees at some larger firms were paid sums of around £10,000 just to defer their training contracts for a year. It's as well to treat this as an unexpected upside to the recession at the time. It was cheaper for these large firms to pay their (relatively numerous) trainees a sum that was much lower than their salaries would have been over the same time period than to take them on as trainees. Since then, more drastic measures have been put in place by firms to reduce their trainee intakes. In some cases trainee recruitment has been frozen altogether, until the economy stabilises. This has had a big impact on the number of training places available. The paid deferral phenomenon looks to have been a one-off – so if you're successful in getting a training contract, make sure you snap it up. Don't set your sights on getting paid to take a year out.

Qualified solicitors

A newly qualified solicitor in a regional firm or smaller commercial practice may expect to earn around £20,000 to £40,000. Starting salaries for newly qualified solicitors in larger commercial firms and those in the City will be from £38,000 to £60,000, with the larger City firms paying £64,000 or more. Salaries at American firms based in the UK will be higher still: some trainees are paid £40,000 or more, while their starting salaries are reputedly as high as £100,000.

There is considerable variation in salary range for more senior or experienced solicitors. Senior solicitors in commercial firms who are not yet at partner level may earn between £40,000 and £90,000 or more, depending on expertise and area of work. Partners may expect to earn from £80,000 to £100,000 or more, with anything up to seven figures being possible, particularly at the larger City and American firms.

Pupil barristers

From September 2011, the minimum salary for pupil barristers is £12,000 for the year of their pupillage, although some barristers' sets may pay a lot more than this, upwards of £50,000 for the year.

This does not look like a lot of money when the outlay on course fees alone – before you even set foot in chambers on the first day of your pupillage – is between £25,000 and £35,000.

Practising barristers

The salaries available to barristers range greatly according to the type of work, and level of experience. As a very rough guide, a barrister may expect to earn between

£12,000 and £90,000 in the first year of qualification. For some criminal work, a junior barrister may earn as little as £50 per day.

As a barrister's level of experience grows, so their clients and cases will increase in value: a barrister with five years' experience may expect to earn between £50,000 and £200,000, while salaries for those with 10 or more years' experience might range from around £65,000 to over £1 million.[3]

Employed barristers will have their salaries determined by their employer according to market rates, with less variation than their self-employed counterparts. Starting salaries may be around the £25,000 mark, in line with other junior-level skilled professional roles, and may rise to more than £130,000, depending on experience and sector.

3

Reality check: is it right for you?

Before we embark on the nitty gritty of qualifications and work, first let's make sure that you're ready to go, and check that nothing will stand in your way at this stage. As we've shown, working in law is extremely competitive, which is why you need to be 100% committed at the outset, to ensure you have the best possible chances of success.

Make your career path realistic

Whichever route you take into law, there will be challenges and, probably, setbacks along the way to qualification. Competition is tough, and it will be rare for an applicant to sail through the various stages of qualification, directly into a training position with no rejected applications, and on to a qualified position as a solicitor or barrister. You may not end up working in the area you had your sights set on initially. However, there is always something to be learned from a setback, which will contribute to your overall experience. In order to maintain efficiency, and to maximise your chances of success (and keep the setbacks to a minimum), you must take the time to assess carefully all the options available to you, and to set and adjust your targets appropriately and realistically as you go, according to your own individual strengths and weaknesses.

Assessing where you're coming from

The way in which you enter the legal profession can have a direct effect on your future experience. Read through the section below to see how this may affect you.

Law graduates

Graduates with qualifying law degrees will have spent three years studying the theory and legal principles that underpin English law. While the course content is similar to that of the Graduate Diploma in Law (GDL), a three-year law degree allows for subjects to be considered in more detail, with more time for consolidation. The availability of alternative routes to law is a relatively recent development. Many people at senior level will have come to the profession after an undergraduate law degree, and some employers also may prefer applicants who have a law degree. The logic is that it is an advantage to have had three years to absorb the subject matter, rather than a few months during a conversion degree. Most employers have no preference as to which route applicants have taken, however.

If you go straight from school to a law degree, and progress through the various stages of training with no gaps, it's possible to become a qualified lawyer in your early to mid-twenties, allowing you to gain those all-important initial years of post-qualification experience relatively early on.

Non-law graduates

Not everyone considers law as an option when deciding which degree to do, while others may only see a legal qualification as an advantage after graduating in a subject other than law, or after working for a while. The conversion route prevents you having to spend six years at university (three in your first subject, then three in law), then another year on a vocational course, and then a further couple of years completing the professional stages of training before you qualify.

The GDL effectively removes two years from the time required for a non-law graduate to qualify, and while it's fair to say that fitting a degree into one year can be a fairly intense experience, the fact that you do not have to take another three-year degree more than makes up for any downsides.

Law degree or conversion?

There is a view that it's impossible to cover and understand adequately the principal legal foundations in one year, and that it's better to have a longer period of exposure to the subject matter of law. Conversely, there is an argument that having experience in addition to a law degree is more useful than having expertise in only one area.

An employer's view: a law firm's HR department gives its perspective

'From an employer's perspective, it may be an advantage for an applicant to have gained knowledge or qualifications in areas other than law. Applicants who have taken the conversion route may be able to offer this, having alternative academic experience, and possibly some work experience too. An essential element of any lawyer's work is having a practical, commercial insight into their clients' work, and previous experience may give you some insight into the commercial context of the legal issues faced in a particular industry or sector. This is particularly the case in specific areas, for example technology or clinical law, if you have an IT or medical degree. On the other hand, those who have done an undergraduate law degree will have detailed knowledge of the course material, and may well have covered one or two subjects in detail, perhaps in a dissertation or project. This can be very useful, particularly if it relates to areas we work in.'

In summary, the GDL/conversion route and three-year law degree route exist to cater for people in different circumstances, so it's not possible to say that one route is 'better' than another – it depends entirely on the individual. The important thing is to make sure you get through either one with the best possible grades, regardless of which route you happen to take, before going on to the Vocational Stage.

Mature applicants

If you are coming to law with experience after school or university, you can set yourself apart by drawing on that experience, and using it to your advantage, at each stage of the qualification process. All previous working experience is valuable, whichever route you take to law, and whichever area you end up working in. Of all the people who have come to law after doing something else, very few have failed to find a legal role they are suited to, and they often find their new legal role more rewarding than what they were doing before. Previous work experience gives you commercial knowledge, develops your interpersonal skills, and may give you some legal knowledge and a working context to fit it to. These things come only with experience, and should be to your advantage. Those coming to law from other backgrounds face different (and sometimes additional) challenges, yet some of the best lawyers around are those who had previous experience before qualification.

Are your academic results sufficient?

Over half of all law degree students who graduated in recent years did so with either a 2.i or a First. This means that at any given time, there is a huge number of people with very good academic credentials in circulation, all looking to fill the vacancies available.

The result of this is that, unfortunately, most employers in law will not consider you unless you have at least a 2.i in your first degree (law or otherwise), and sometimes at least a commendation or equivalent at the Legal Practice Course (LPC) or the Bar Professional Training Course (BPTC; formerly the Bar Vocational Course) level. If this wasn't bad enough, many employers – especially mid- to large-sized commercial firms – will request all your exam grades from GCSE onwards, including assessments and marks gained during your degree, and during any of the legal courses you have done so far.

The important thing to remember is that employers see a lot of high-quality applications. They are offering applicants a rare and desirable opportunity to progress in their chosen career, and do not owe the applicants anything. With so many people for employers to choose from, you need to make sure that your application is as strong as it possibly can be, to give an employer no reason to reject it at first glance. We will look at applications in much more detail in Chapter 6.

To make matters worse, many employers (particularly law firms) only accept applications online, and will not allow applicants to progress unless they first confirm that they have at least a 2.i degree and a minimum of 320 UCAS points at A level (or equivalent). If you don't meet these minimum requirements, the system will not permit you to go further. There are things you can do in this situation, however, and we will look at these in Chapter 6 also.

Do not be discouraged if you have one or two blips on your CV. There are ways to approach this, and even to turn them to your advantage when making applications, which we will look at later.

Thinking about your finances

Financial aspects of further study

Tuition fees vary from provider to provider, and you should check the prospectus of your chosen university or college for up-to-date details of course fees for the courses you intend to enrol on.

The cost of conversion courses ranges from around £3,100 (part-time) to over £9,000 (full-time) – and remember, you can only enrol if you have a first degree, so you will already have racked up the costs of a few years at university before you start the conversion course.

The LPC starts at around £8,000 (or £4,000 part-time) and can go up to more than £13,000 for some full-time courses in London.

The BPTC fees can be as high as an eye-watering £16,500. When you consider that each of these courses is only one year long (full-time), or two years part-time, the financial outlay on fees is significant.

The Law Society of England and Wales estimates that the overall cost of a degree and/or the GDL and LPC, including living expenses, will be between £25,000 and £50,000. Living expenses vary greatly on a case-by-case basis, but according to the National Union of Students' figures,[4] the average cost of student living for the academic year 2010/11 was £16,613 in London, with living costs outside London being approximately £1,090 lower.

Funding

Sources of funding that are available to all students include student loans, local authority maintenance grants (which, unlike student loans, do not have to be paid back), bank loans and professional or career development loans.

The Law Society offers financial assistance towards the cost of LPC course fees for future solicitors through a Diversity Access Scheme (the Bursary Scheme previously offered is no longer available, althrough applicants who were eligible for the bursary will also be eligible for the Diversity Access Scheme). The scheme offers financial support to individuals in a position of serious financial hardship and is aimed at exceptional, aspiring entrants. Successful applicants are also provided with mentoring and work experience opportunities. The application process is strict, and only a small number of awards are made relative to the number of applicants each year. More information on these, and other schemes, is available on the Law Society's junior lawyers website.[5]

You should check with your course provider if they offer any scholarships or other assistance, as many offer generous scholarships across many of the courses they provide. Overseas students may be eligible for assistance through the British Council, and there are various other scholarships set up privately to assist applicants who satisfy certain eligibility criteria.

For barristers, the four Inns of Court (Inner Temple, Middle Temple, Gray's Inn and Lincoln's Inn) offer scholarships to BPTC and GDL students. Contact each Inn for information on how and when to apply.

Financial aspects of training

The illustrations above demonstrate just how much of a financial commitment is required in order to gain the entry-level qualifications to law. Even in the event that you secure funding from a firm or chambers to cover some or even all of your course fees, it may still be a struggle to make ends meet. This is particularly the case if you are studying full-time, and are therefore unable to find paid work that adequately covers your living expenses.

Budgeting

It is critical that you plan each step of the qualification process carefully well before you start. You need to work out a detailed budget for exactly what the fees and other expenses will be for each qualification you are planning. This will allow you to come to a balanced conclusion as to whether you feel the amount you will have to spend will be justified at each stage, given the lack of guarantees of a job at the end of it all.

Even if your ultimate objective is to become a fully qualified solicitor or barrister, it is well worth treating each stage of qualification as its own individual unit. Each level of qualification has value in its own right, and will open doors to areas of legal work that would otherwise be shut.

Timing and managing your qualification progress

If you have yet to secure a training contract or pupillage, having completed your LPC or BPTC, you may find yourself in a position where there will be a gap between the end of the LPC or BPTC and the start of your training contract or pupillage. It will be a disappointment not to be able to progress directly from one stage to the next, but this can be turned to your advantage. A year or two in a part-qualified legal role will build on the skills gained at each level of qualification. It cannot be overestimated how important practical legal experience is, particularly when approaching prospective employers for training positions – being forced to take some time between each stage of qualification may in fact be the perfect opportunity to gain this experience.

Working in a part-qualified legal role between one stage of training and the next has a number of other advantages. It will help ease the financial strain, and possibly allow you to save for the next set of course fees or living expenses. Your contact base will increase greatly through the real-life work experience your position will offer you, and a year or two of 'proper' legal work also gives you the opportunity to prove your worth to your employer over a reasonably long period of time. Even if there are no opportunities to go up to the next level with them, your colleagues will almost certainly know people in other firms, chambers or companies who may be able to offer you something. Your work experience will show you off as a credible candidate, with a good level of understanding of the areas of law that you are looking to progress into.

If you have secured a training position, it will be easier for you to map out the likely route that you will take to qualification, and to plan your time accordingly. Even so, you need to keep a careful eye on your finances.

> You should be aware that time limits apply to the validity of some academic and vocational qualifications. For solicitors, the Academic Stage qualifications (law degree or conversion) will be valid for seven years, while there is no expiry date for LPC. The BPTC is valid for five years after completion.

The bottom line

Is (your chosen area of) law right for you, and do you have a realistic chance of succeeding?

The only guarantee that you can bank on at the start of your legal training is that it will take a lot of effort, time and financial outlay to progress through each stage of the qualification process. This is the case regardless of which direction you want your legal career to take. When assessing your chances of success, a good starting point is to look at your Academic Stage and Vocational Stage qualifications as one set of credentials in their own right, and take the professional training (training contract or pupillage) as a separate process altogether.

The academic courses are rigorous, time-consuming and costly. It is, however, entirely within your control as to how well you perform. Assuming you have the necessary credentials to get onto the courses initially, it will be down to you to manage your time, put the work in, and make sure you get the highest grades you can. You are responsible, which means your fate is not subject to factors beyond your control (except perhaps the inevitable bad exam paper!). Even if it looks unlikely, for whatever reason, that you will progress through to full qualification, your legal qualifications will always be on your CV, and will always be useful.

Training contracts and pupillages are notoriously difficult to obtain. The number of training places has always been fewer than the number of applicants to fill them, but the situation has worsened since the recession of 2009/10. There has been a decline in the number of training contracts and pupillages available but a steady increase in the number of people applying for them. Every application you make will find itself among many other equally (or more) convincing applications. You will then have to get through interviews and further assessments, where other factors will come into play and will influence your chances of success, just like in any other job application.

If you assess what your options might be with the skills and experience gained at each stage of the qualification process (as well as viewing the process as a whole), you will be at an advantage over those whose only goal is becoming a fully qualified solicitor or barrister. If you set your sights on full qualification only, you are limiting your options, and greatly increasing the likelihood of disappointment. We will look at ways to deal with the challenges to be overcome during the application process in Chapter 11, but you will help yourself enormously if you plan for contingencies along the way, by thinking flexibly from the start, and by having realistic expectations.

fact

To be a successful lawyer of tomorrow you need the best training available today

Our highly structured programmes are unlike others. Taught by qualified lawyers using a high proportion of face-to-face tuition and supported by cutting-edge multi-media tools, our training will hone your professional skills so that from day one you will think and act as a lawyer. That's why we find more work for future lawyers than any other law school.

If you're serious about law, qualify with the leaders in law.

The full range of courses to prepare you for your legal career: GDL/LPC/BPTC/LL.M Flexible full-time, part-time and S-mode options available nationwide

The College of **Law**
believing in your future

 To find out more join the Future Lawyers Netw at **college-of-law.co.uk/futurelawyers54** or call **0800 289997**

Profile: The College of Law

Maximising your chances of success

Law is an ever-popular career choice, and competition to enter the profession is high even at the best of times. In the current economic climate you need to keep one step ahead of the competition, in order to maximise your chances of success.

To help you do so, The College of Law has developed a free, online Student Employability Programme (StEP), taking you through the following 10 key steps or stages to a career in law:

Step 1: Understand the legal market

What do you really know about the legal market you're interested in joining? Step 1 takes you through the two main arms of the profession (solicitors and barristers), different types of legal employer, and the main practice areas. You can keep up to date with changes to the legal profession, ranging from the Legal Services Act to globalisation; from emerging markets to the role of technology in the delivery of legal services.

Step 2: Assess your employability

Find out what legal employers are looking for. Many legal recruiters expect a consistently good academic record; relevant work experience; commercial awareness; and a range of skills and abilities such as oral and written communication, numerical and verbal reasoning, negotiating, and being a team player.

Step 3: Plan your career

You will make an easier transition to a career in law if you plan your career properly, as targeting your efforts will save you a good deal of time and effort in the long run.

As many law firms and chambers recruit two to three years in advance, you need to start planning early, as you will be juggling three different 'timetables': an academic timetable, a 'work experience' timetable and the recruitment timetable.

Step 4: Research employers

Legal recruiters tell us that the single biggest reason that applications fail is because the candidate has failed to research employers and target applications properly. We show you how to 'market' yourself to a recruiter by making targeted approaches which show that you understand what the organisation is about, and what they're looking for in their recruits.

Step 5: Gain experience and make contact

Employers want to see that you are committed to a career in law, and have a real understanding of what a career in law entails. The best way to demonstrate your commitment and understanding is by securing legal work experience, and this step shows you how.

If you're off to the Bar, then you'll need to arrange a mini-pupillage or two. If you are intending to be a solicitor, many of the larger firms are increasingly treating their work experience schemes as an integral part of the recruitment process, and competition for formal 'vacation schemes' is fierce.

Step 6: Draft a legal-specific CV and covering letter

Make sure that you target your CV to each individual employer you are applying to (this is where your research in Step 4 comes in!). Identify what the employer wants, and think about how your unique blend of skills and experience meets those requirements. While your CV must be professional, easy to read, and no more than two sides long, remember that style is no substitute for content, which is why Step 5 is essential.

Step 7: Make convincing applications

As with CVs, targeting each answer to the particular recruiter is key: it's easy to spot 'generic' applications and it doesn't impress! A good application form can take many hours to complete, and it is best to start early, leave the form, and come back to it with fresh eyes. Don't leave your application to the last minute before submitting, though; employers have been known to bring forward a closing date if they are inundated with applications – and do keep a copy!

Step 8: Prepare for interview

The old adage 'failing to prepare is preparing to fail' should be your motto here. As a basic checklist you should: re-read your application form/CV and anticipate likely questions; go back over your research (student directories, legal press online, and the website); and prepare a few questions to ask the employer. If you are able to access a careers service, book an appointment for a mock interview.

Step 9: Prepare for assessment centres

Some firms (usually the larger ones) hold 'assessment centres'. You will be given details of what to expect, but they usually consist of an interview, a presentation, and a range of tests and activities, such as an 'in-tray' exercise, a group exercise, situational judgement tests or psychometric tests looking at your verbal or numerical reasoning. This may sound daunting, but you can practise many of these tests online; and good old common sense will stand you in good stead.

Step 10: Manage your career

Finally, not only should you plan your career, you should also actively manage your career. Constantly reassess the early decisions and career plan you made – as you progress through your research and the recruitment process you will probably define and re-define your plan many times. In a competitive market you may need to be proactive and flexible, and adjust your plan accordingly.

Maximise your chances – join the Future Lawyers Network and access the 10 StEP programme for yourself: www.college-of-law.co.uk/futurelawyers54.

PART 2
How the legal world works

4

Areas of law

The seven foundation subjects

Every lawyer in England and Wales begins by mastering the seven foundation subjects, which together make up the basis of English law. These are the most fundamental aspects of English law, and while they may appear relatively abstract and unrelated, they all link to each other in different ways, and can appear together in any number of different contexts. They are all equally important at the start, even if some of them may appear to have no possible bearing on your future career, or may seem particularly obscure. One or other of these legal areas will apply to virtually every legal situation. As such, the foundation areas crop up time and again in your career, no matter which direction you take. We will look at how these areas of law interact with each other, and relate to particular areas of legal work, later in the chapter.

The foundation subjects are:

- contract law

- public law (constitutional, administrative and human rights law)

- criminal law

- equity and trusts

- European Union law

- land law

- tort law.

They are taught as separate subjects on all law degree or conversion courses. As your career progresses you will see how they cross over, but for now, here is a summary of what each foundation subject is all about. It is important to note that there are differences between the legal systems of England and Wales, and the systems of the other countries that make up the UK: Scotland and Northern Ireland. While there is a good deal of similarity between the systems, this book deals with qualification under the law of England and Wales.

Contract law

Contract law deals with the principles that govern agreements between parties that can be legally enforced. Contracts are formed all the time – every time you buy something or use most kinds of service, you will have entered a formal contract. Contract law therefore affects almost every aspect of our lives, in one way or another. Contracts come about in many ways (for example, a contract does not have to be in writing), and certain elements need to be present before a legally enforceable contract can be said to exist.

In addition to understanding the requirements for forming a contract, the extent to which a contract can be limited or extended in scope is also important. Can a party exempt certain things from being included in a contract? What if this might be considered unfair to the other party to the same contract? The study of contract law also looks at how the courts will analyse points of law where disputes have arisen between parties, and the courts' ability to step in to resolve the dispute through remedies for breach of contract.

Constitutional and administrative law

Constitutional law is the foundation for allowing society to be legitimately governed. You will look at the background and sources of the English constitutional system as it exists today, as well as the main constitutional concepts:

- the rule of law (the concept that no person is above the law)

- separation of powers (the status of government being separate from the monarchy, both of which are in turn separate from the judiciary)

- parliamentary sovereignty (where the decisions of Parliament are the supreme legal authority).

Administrative law takes the principles of constitutional government and applies them to society. This includes the rights of individual citizens within the state apparatus, and covers human rights, freedom of association and assembly, freedom of expression and privacy. Police powers over the citizen make up an important part of this area of law, including issues such as police powers of arrest, detention and search, and citizens' rights granted under statute, such as the Criminal Justice and Police Act 2001.

Judicial review is another key element of administrative law. This is the process available to citizens to challenge the validity of a decision made by a public body (perhaps a government department, local council or other state institution) through the courts. As the judiciary is independent of government, judges are in a position to impose remedies where necessary. Specific criteria apply in challenging a decision through the judicial review process; these are looked at by reference to cases and decisions made over the years.

Criminal law

Criminal law is the subject of news headlines, courtroom dramas and crime documentaries, but what is 'crime'? This area of law concentrates on the measures in place to control society through an analysis of the key principles that make up 'criminal law', and a review of certain offences and their consequences. The subject matter is gritty and often uncomfortable, but fundamental questions are raised as to what should be considered a 'crime' and as to the morality of society's right to impose punishment on its own members.

The elements required to constitute a crime are the building blocks of criminal law. These start with the basic requirement for there to be a combination of 'guilty act' or *actus reus*, and 'guilty mind' or *mens rea* on the part of the offender. Elements of the most common offences against the person and against property are also covered: non-sexual offences such as wounding, murder, theft, deception and criminal damage and sexual offences such as rape.

Next, what happens when a crime has been committed, and the person who committed the crime has been identified? Treatment of the offender is considered, and includes offenders' liability, their capacity or incapacity to commit the offence, how the law treats attempted crime, and the defences available to those accused of certain offences.

Equity and trusts law

Equity is, very broadly, a system of rights and remedies that exists alongside other areas of law. The purpose of equity is to serve the interests of justice and fairness in cases where other legal remedies have not been able to do so adequately. Equitable remedies can be available in situations that relate to ownership of property, and are particularly important in the creation and implementation of trusts.

This may at first seem to be a technical and obscure area of law, but in fact it is applied in all kinds of day-to-day situations: gifts, charities, pensions, investments and insurance are all areas that fall within the scope of the law of equity and trusts, and this area of law plays a vital role in most people's everyday lives.

European Union law

There are 27 Member States in the European Union, all of which are governed by one unifying system of laws to encourage and maintain certain rights and freedoms for the wider benefit of all Member States. This system shapes Member States' interaction with their neighbouring territories, particularly regarding trade and commerce. European Union law covers the historical development of the European

Union and its institutions, and how European law is implemented in the national courts of Member States.

The key areas of European law considered in detail are:

- competition law

- free movement of goods and workers

- freedom of establishment of businesses and services

- freedom from discrimination.

Land law

Land law is considered by many law students to be particularly useful in its practical application in day-to-day life. Whether you are buying or selling a flat or house, renting, or living at home, knowledge of land law is an extremely useful tool in understanding property ownership, in terms of what you may or may not do with property, and how property may be affected by the rights of others.

The course does not deal with the technical aspects of conveyancing. This is practical legal work usually done by solicitors, and is therefore covered on the solicitors' Legal Practice Course (see Chapter 7).

Land law as a foundation subject deals with the main legal concepts governing the ownership and use of land:

- registered and unregistered land

- freehold and leasehold

- obligations of landlord and tenant

- obligations under leasehold covenants

- trusts over land, licences, and third-party rights in land (mortgages and charges, easements and freehold covenants).

Law of tort

The law of tort is used to impose liability and remedies for a broad range of acts resulting in 'harm' to related parties, but which may not be covered by liability in contract, or by other areas of law. Tort is a strand of law that has developed through the courts rather than through legislation and statute. As a result, much of the material covered is based in case law, requiring analysis of factual and legal points that have arisen and been decided by the courts in many different contexts.

A fundamental area of tort law is the concept of negligence, and the existence of a duty of care between neighbouring parties. This is a relatively recent legal concept, as industrial progress in the nineteenth century increased cases of death and injury to members of society. With this came a need to develop the law to protect society by balancing the benefits of industrial and economic progress with the risk of harm or damage to people and property. As a result, case law developed and consolidated into the legal framework of tort law, to allow cases in which harm had been suffered to be decided with some consistency.

Various aspects of negligence are considered, including duty of care and breach of duty, economic loss, psychiatric illness, and the liability of employers and occupiers of premises. Negligence is probably the broadest area of tort, while trespass, defamation, nuisance and aspects of consumer protection also fall within it. Tort matters are usually contentious in nature, involving a claimant and defendant, so the various defences and remedies available are also looked at.

How legal work relates to what you are taught

Before we get into the specifics of qualification, it is worth having a look now at how the legal theory generally relates to legal practice. A good way to explain the relationships between what you learn at the Academic and Vocational stages of qualification, and how this relates to legal work, is to look at some example scenarios.

These scenarios are taken from real-life situations, and while they provide only a small snapshot of the kinds of legal problems that may occur in practice, they are a useful illustration of how some of the different areas of law interact and come into play in different situations. These are the kinds of issues you will come across as you work in any legal environment, and are an indication of what to expect not only in legal practice, but also perhaps in interviews or applications.

Scenario 1

A building company finishes a large development for a client several months later than the agreed date, and the work is dangerously substandard.

Some of the legal issues involved are listed below.

- Contract law: What were the terms of the agreement in place between the company and the client? This will define what was agreed, and the options available to both parties.

- Property law: Aspects of property and construction law will come into play in analyzing the extent to which the finished project is, or is not, fit for purpose.

- Tort: If the poorly completed work is dangerous, might the building company be liable to anyone who might be injured as a result of its failure to complete the work adequately?

- Litigation and strategy: There will need to be careful consideration of the strategy to take, depending on which side you are advising. Is settlement an option? Can the work be redone or remedied in some way? Would financial compensation be available? Would it be an adequate remedy for the problem? What if the client had contractual obligations of its own to sell or rent the development to a third party, but has been unable to do so?

Scenario 2

An employee is sacked from his job for alleging that his manager's son, also an employee, had been stealing money from the company.

Some of the legal issues involved are listed below.

- Criminal law: There are allegations of theft – how might these be pursued? By whom? What sort of problems are likely to be faced if a criminal investigation takes place?

- Contract law: The employee and employer are both bound by the terms of the contract of employment – what does that contract say?

- Employment law: Eligibility to pursue a legal claim through the employment tribunals is subject to criteria which would need to be satisfied. The claims and remedies available are prescribed by employment legislation, which in turn is shaped by European and constitutional legal principles. This might include whistleblowing: does the possibility that the employee is acting in the public interest help him in any way?

- Litigation and strategy: Who are you acting for? The employee, the manager, the son, the company? Should the employee claim against the employer by litigation in an employment tribunal? How much money is the claim worth? Are there any other ways to resolve the situation? What would be the benefits and downsides to each option? Might another route to settlement be a better option?

Scenario 3

A company director wants to merge his company with another.

In a situation like this, some of the legal issues might include the following.

- Property law: Does either company own or lease premises? How will ownership be allocated following the merger? Will the current premises still be required? Will any property need to be sold, bought or leased?

- Employment law: Are staff employed by either company? How may their positions be affected by the merger? What are the employees' rights and the employer's obligations in a situation like this?

- Company and corporate law: How would the shareholdings be allocated, to ensure control of each company is maintained as agreed between the parties? What documentation needs to be prepared? What other administrative work or registrations need to be done? What is the proposed timescale for the merger? Will this impact on how the process is to be managed by the legal teams involved?

- EU and international law: What if the other company is based outside the UK, perhaps in the EU? If both companies operate in the same sector, might there be competition issues if they were to merge?

Scenario 4

A couple decide that they want to buy a flat occupied until recently by an elderly resident, who has since died. They would need to consider the following legal questions.

- Probate and administration of estates: Who now owns the property? If it was the resident, did she have a will in place? Have executors been appointed, and probate granted? Are they in a position to sell the property?

- Property law: Is the flat freehold or leasehold? Are any parts of the property shared with anyone else? Are there any restrictions on how they might use the flat? How will their ownership of the flat be shared, once they take possession of it? Do the couple require a mortgage? If so, will it be in one of their names, or both? What are the implications of this?

- Contract and tort: What if the couple moves in, and find that the surveyor they used did not pick up on some important defects to the flat, which will cost a lot of money to remedy? What provisions are in their contract with the surveyor? Might the surveyor have worked negligently?

- Litigation and strategy: As with some of the other scenarios, the couple would need advice on which options are available to them if a dispute arose, and if they wished to be compensated for any losses incurred, as would other parties involved in the sale.

Contentious or non-contentious?

In any of these scenarios, a solicitor may be acting for either party. This would be the case for the transactional, non-contentious arrangements, or if a dispute were to occur. If a dispute has arisen, input from a barrister may be required to manage the litigation or dispute resolution process. If this were to happen, the legal team would need to consider additional points.

Will it be necessary to prepare for a court or tribunal hearing? The pros and cons of this approach will need to be weighed up, as court preparation and procedures are time-consuming and expensive.

Is it likely that a settlement might be reached? This is always an option, and is often better than going all the way to court. If so, which dispute resolution method might be best? Mediation? Arbitration? There are different rules and procedures for each, which will need to be considered in light of the facts of the case, and explained to the client to help them decide upon the best strategy.

We will look at this in more detail in Chapter 5.

Summary

You can see that, while the foundations of law can be viewed as separate entities in theory, when it comes to real-life legal problems, there will almost always be several areas of law involved, each overlapping with the others, depending on the nature of the matter. Certain areas may appear together frequently and may be relatively straightforward to deal with. Other situations may place more rarely seen areas of law together, which may pose a challenge to finding an adequate solution. This may require more specialist input, from a specialist lawyer, barrister, or perhaps patent attorney, or other adviser operating in a particular area of law. Keep these different disciplines and areas in mind as you go through your training, as opportunities within them may expand your target area for potential career options.

And where do you fit into all this as a working lawyer? We look at this in more detail in the next chapter.

5

Legal roles and lawyers' areas of practice

The legal profession, as we have seen, is generally divided into two parts: solicitors and barristers. While solicitors and barristers both start off studying the same foundation subjects at the Academic Stage, they are each required to do different vocational courses (the LPC or BPTC), and will go on to do entirely different professional training (solicitors' training contracts, and barristers' pupillages). So, what are the differences between the two professions?

Solicitors

A solicitor is anyone who has gone through one of the recognised routes to qualification, and who is, or has been, in possession of a Solicitors Regulation Authority (SRA) practising certificate. Once the various stages of training are all complete, a solicitor must apply to have his or her name entered on the SRA roll of solicitors, and apply for their first practising certificate in order to become qualified and eligible to practise as a solicitor.

The solicitor's role is to work directly with the client, taking their instructions, advising the client on legal aspects to a matter, and managing certain administrative aspects of matters as they progress. Importantly, solicitors are in a position to act on their client's behalf, as an attorney, which a barrister is not. A solicitor will be responsible for reviewing and drafting legal documentation (contracts, deeds, witness statements, pleadings, etc.), preparing evidence, and liaising with barristers where necessary, in disputes or litigation proceedings.

Private practice and in-house

Solicitors will be employed either in private practice law firms or in-house in other organisations. Those working in private practice will often develop expertise in certain areas of law, or certain areas of commercial or other activity, and will be particularly familiar with the kinds of legal problems that occur in those contexts.

Note that if a firm is a partnership, then it is not a 'company', as it does not comply with the formal requirements of being a company. Referring to a solicitors' firm as a 'company' is, technically, incorrect.

Solicitors working in-house can be required to work on any legal issue that their employer may come into contact with. Issues may concern the core business or activity of the organisation, or any number of other legal problems, perhaps in employment, dealing with a lease of premises, corporate matters such as finance arrangements, or a company merger or acquisition. No solicitor is expected to know all there is to know about such a wide array of law, so in-house solicitors frequently use the services of private practice lawyers to deal with issues requiring specialist input. If a legal issue is particularly complex, obscure or unusual, a private practice solicitor may in turn consult a barrister for additional expert advice, as necessary.

Contentious and non-contentious work

Solicitors' work will generally be contentious or non-contentious in nature, and these categories are often used to describe the nature of any matter a solicitor is working on.

Contentious work

Contentious work is concerned with the prevention and resolution of legal disputes. Whenever something goes wrong with a legal arrangement between any parties, a contentious situation arises. There are several methods available to resolve disputes other than going to court, and the parties will generally want to avoid the cost, stress and potential negative publicity of going all the way to formal court litigation. However, this will be the final option if all other routes to resolution fail. The solicitor's job is to give the best advice to their client on the legal issues, and to set out the options available to reach an appropriate resolution of the dispute.

Contentious work centres on the legal issues behind a case, analysing the facts in detail to ascertain the client's position, and analysing the opposing party's position to assess the merits of both sides' arguments. Excellent working knowledge of the law and the ability to apply the law to the facts of a contentious matter are essential. Negotiation skills are also crucial when working with the opposition's legal representatives. The same goes for the skills involved in dealing with clients, who may be under considerable stress as a result of being caught up in a legal dispute.

Since the processes of dispute resolution are formal and prescribed, detailed knowledge of the various procedures is also required, to formulate the best strategy for a given matter, and to guide a case through to a successful conclusion.

In the past, solicitors were obliged to use a barrister for advocacy in cases other than relatively minor criminal cases in the magistrates' courts, and lower-value or less complex civil cases in county courts. While the solicitors' and barristers' professions remain as two distinct areas of practice, solicitors are now able to become 'solicitor advocates', allowing them to represent clients directly in any court or tribunal, without incurring the additional expense of hiring a barrister. Training is available for solicitors wishing to qualify as solicitor advocates – see Chapter 10 for more details.

Non-contentious work

Non-contentious work is characterised by advising on aspects of legal arrangements being put in place between parties, to ensure legal and other regulatory compliance. The solicitor's role is to ensure that legal matters are managed properly, and agreements are constructed in such a way that if a dispute were to arise, appropriate protection for the client has been factored into the agreement. In some ways, non-contentious legal work can be viewed as 'prevention', while contentious work and dispute resolution are more akin to a 'cure'.

Non-contentious work involves managing the administrative aspects of matters, such as checking through all necessary paperwork, maintaining documentation, or ensuring that registrations and forms are filed correctly and on time. This may not always require detailed legal knowledge, but requires a solicitor's input to ensure that all legal obligations are covered and are understood by the client.

Solicitors are often required to negotiate on the client's behalf, to ensure that the client receives the best possible terms. While no formal legal dispute may have occurred, it is a myth that complex, challenging and sometimes heated negotiations only occur in the context of disputes and litigation. The stakes can be high for both parties to a commercial deal or any other legal agreement, and there can sometimes be very little difference in pressure and excitement between negotiations in a non-contentious or contentious context.

Barristers

A barrister is an independent lawyer specialising in advocacy, litigation, and giving expert, objective advice on specific areas of law. They are most often engaged in contentious matters, generally leaving non-contentious legal work to solicitors. They usually take instructions from solicitors rather than from clients directly, leaving the administrative side of matters and direct client contact for the solicitors to manage.

The barrister's profession has a long history, and has developed into the expert profession it is today after being shaped by developments to the courts system, and litigation practice in general, over several hundred years. This is sometimes reflected in the language used within it, and in the traditions that continue to be observed. For example, a barrister can only call him or herself a 'barrister' if they have been 'called to the Bar' by an Inn of Court, meaning that they have completed the Academic Stage of legal training (a law degree or conversion course), are a member of a particular Inn and, from September 2010, have completed pupillage. 'Bar' is the original word used collectively to describe all qualified barristers, while the 'Inns of Court' were originally private buildings where lawyers would live and work. Today, the Inns are professional organisations which regulate the barristers' profession and provide educational, research and other essential resources. Barristers are referred to as 'counsel'; this term is used much more commonly than the word 'barrister' in day-to-day legal business.

Qualified barristers are generally self-employed, but often share offices, administration teams and other services in 'chambers' with other barristers specialising in compatible areas of law. Barristers working from chambers are referred to as 'tenants', and may only become tenants after completing a pupillage. Within chambers, senior barristers often use the services of more junior tenant barristers or pupil barristers to assist on larger matters, but as barristers working from chambers are self-employed, the decision of who works with who will be made according to the skills and experience of particular individuals. There is nothing to stop barristers working with colleagues from other chambers, if this would be best for a particular matter.

Court appearances are probably the best known, and perhaps the highest-profile, aspect of a barrister's work. This involves putting submissions to the judge, guiding the judge and, where applicable, the jury through evidence and legal points, and responding to the opposing counsel's argument. The objective is of course to make as persuasive a case as possible, and to obtain a ruling in the barrister's client's favour.

Barristers are involved in a number of other areas, as well as appearing 'on their feet' in court. Some of these are described below.

Written opinions

Solicitors may require expert advice on a particular legal point. Advice is usually given in writing, and is referred to as 'counsel's opinion'. Counsel's opinion may be sought in a contentious matter, for advice on litigation strategy, or on how the law might be interpreted in the context of the facts of a particular matter. Barristers may also be consulted in non-contentious matters, perhaps to clarify how particular areas of law may affect a commercial transaction, or when complex or unusual facts make interpretation of the law particularly difficult.

Conferences

When a barrister meets with the solicitor who has instructed him or her, perhaps also with the solicitor's client, the meeting is referred to as a 'conference'. The solicitor will usually provide the barrister with the background materials to the matter under discussion, and, in conference, the barrister will go through the various issues with the solicitor, and will advise on relevant legal or procedural points. It is generally the case that prior to litigation, one or two conferences with counsel will be needed. If a case goes to trial, there is often ongoing consultation with counsel, before, during and after the hearing.

Negotiation

When counsel has been instructed by each party to a dispute, it will frequently be appropriate for them to negotiate terms to reach a possible settlement. This might be the case when a matter reaches trial, if it becomes evident that settlement might be better for both parties, instead of continuing the trial. This would avoid the risk of an unpredictable decision, which may have a negative impact on both sides.

Drafting documentation

Barristers are often instructed to draft documents in the context of litigation, such as particulars of a claim or defence, applications and other court documents. There is sometimes no formal requirement for a barrister to draft these documents, but their input may save time and have other advantages in terms of efficient case management.

Legal research

The law is constantly changing as new legislation is brought in, and as cases are decided, and this affects all areas of legal practice. Barristers keep fully up to date with developments in the law affecting their areas of expertise through regular legal research. Junior barristers gain valuable experience early on in their careers through assisting more senior counsel with legal research in complex areas of law, while also researching the law on matters they are handling themselves.

Employed barristers

In a similar way to solicitors, barristers can work in-house for specific organisations, including law firms, and around 20% of qualified barristers work in employed practice. A barrister working in-house will be referred to as an 'employed barrister' rather than a 'practising barrister'. Historically, once a barrister had completed the Bar Vocational Course (now replaced by the BPTC) and been called to the Bar, they could become employed barristers right away, without completing a pupillage under a practising barrister. If not employed or taking up tenancy, the term 'non-practising barrister' was used to describe their status, but this is no longer the case. The recent introduction of the Bar Professional Training Course (BPTC), and revised professional regulations, means that the term 'barrister' is now reserved only for those who have gone through all stages of training, including pupillage.

Barristers' practice areas

Barristers work in all areas of the law, and while there is considerable crossover, their practice areas are usually divided into the following categories, with most barristers specialising in perhaps two or three areas:

- criminal law

- commercial law and chancery

- common law

- employment law

- family law

- personal injury and clinical negligence

- constitutional and administrative law

- European law.

The BPTC is structured according to these areas, so take a look at Chapter 7 to get a good idea of how the practice areas and BPTC course materials relate to each other.

Differences between a solicitor and a barrister

There are a number of characteristics that separate solicitors and barristers, once they have achieved their respective qualifications. We mentioned earlier that, in most cases, barristers are not instructed by clients directly, and do not act as a client's attorney. They take instructions from solicitors, and will generally deal only through the solicitor.

Here are some other main differences between the two professions.

- The solicitor is responsible for paying the barrister's fees, although fees will be passed on by the solicitor to the client.

- On qualification, a barrister is permitted to conduct advocacy in all courts and tribunals. A solicitor's qualification does not permit this in itself. In order to conduct advocacy in higher courts (known as 'Higher Rights of Audience'), a solicitor is required to obtain additional qualifications.

- Barristers are experts in dispute resolution, and specialise in the practical conduct of litigation in and out of court. A solicitor will be required to ensure that the barrister has all the factual and other details from the client, allowing the barrister to focus on the strategy and procedure of litigation, as well as the courtroom advocacy. Not all solicitors deal with litigation and dispute resolution.

- As we have seen, barristers work independently, grouping together to share certain offices in 'chambers', and to offer a range of related legal services as a 'set'. Solicitors may work alone as sole practitioners, but more frequently work in partnerships or as employees in firms, with shared responsibilities.

- Another difference between solicitors and barristers is how they are dressed for work in court: barristers are quite distinctive in wigs and gowns, while solicitors will usually wear a conventional suit (although solicitor advocates now have their own formal dress that is equivalent to a barrister's).

Other legal roles, in addition to solicitors and barristers

Many people come to law intending to qualify as a solicitor or barrister, but find that it is not possible to progress directly from one stage of qualification to the next. Others come to law intending to work in a particular area from the start, without intending to tick off all the various stages required for full qualification as a solicitor or barrister.

For most solicitors' and barristers' training positions, applications can be submitted only once a year. It is common therefore for people who have not yet secured a training contract or pupillage by the time they finish their LPC or BPTC to fill a year or two with legal work which builds their experience, and puts the qualifications they have to good use. Luckily, the law is such a broad area that there are always positions to be filled by part-qualified lawyers. For those with no formal legal training, there are opportunities to gain experience and qualifications while working (see Chapter 8).

Below are some of the more common part-qualified and specialist roles, all of which can offer excellent insight into legal practice, helping you gain valuable points for your CV, or which can offer plenty of career options in themselves.

Part-qualified roles

Paralegal or legal assistant

Paralegal work is usually either offered through private practice solicitors' firms, or in-house in the legal department of other organisations. While no formal qualifications are needed to work as a paralegal, most firms will usually prefer applicants with at least a law degree or conversion degree, and usually an LPC or BPTC qualification too.

The majority of the work is spent assisting with practical aspects of matters being managed by more senior lawyers, potentially in any area of law. A paralegal working in litigation will manage the production and administration of case documents and bundles (sets of formal documents and files used in litigation). They will liaise with court and tribunal staff, barristers and their clerks on important administrative matters, and might assist with drafting and proofreading particulars of claims, witness statements and other court documents. Paralegal work in a non-contentious capacity might involve anything from drafting contracts or other agreements, assisting with legal research, taking and preparing notes in client meetings, to writing articles or dealing with forms or registrations for Companies House or the Land Registry.

Paralegal work offers excellent hands-on experience and insight into day-to-day legal work. It is often seen as a vital bridge between academic legal study and practical legal work, and can be the best way to get an idea of what you might experience as your legal career progresses. Most legal employers see experience gained as a paralegal or legal assistant as a very positive attribute on a CV. Working as a paralegal can introduce you to the firm or chambers you may wish to apply to, making you a 'known quantity' and possibly putting you towards the top of the list for future positions that may come up, including training contracts or pupillages. This experience also broadens your range of subject matter to draw from in interviews and applications. We will look at how this experience can be put to use in getting a training position in Chapter 11.

Case study

Katherine Pymont worked as a paralegal, and is now a trainee solicitor in the London firm Kingsley Napley

After getting very good grades on the GDL and LPC, my first legal role was as a legal assistant in the firm's regulatory and professional discipline department, assisting with regulatory prosecution work. This included consideration of papers received on instruction from clients, meeting with and taking statements from witnesses, preparing witness statements, drafting correspondence and liaising with witnesses and with the client. The work was challenging, interesting and varied, and no two days were the same.

One of the best things about working as a legal assistant at Kingsley Napley was the level of responsibility that I was given. I was expected to run my own case load, with my opinion being valued by the lawyer responsible for each case. The experience provided invaluable experience and I am soon to complete a training contract with the firm. I am sure that my time as a legal assistant contributed to securing my training contract.

Daniel Turnbull, partner at City firm Stewarts Law LLP, explains how paralegal work is valued, and helps with securing a training position:

'At my firm we advertise internally for training contracts, and trainees are often recruited from our team of paralegals. We have a unique approach in that we have approximately one paralegal per fee earner. This means there is usually quite a *number of paralegals in our firm, many of whom are looking for training contracts. This is advantageous both for the firm, and for the staff themselves, and the system works well. The paralegals are very motivated, and they know that if they work well they will be rewarded. If they don't get a training contract on the first attempt, they can take a second or third opportunity to get there. I look around my office and see paralegals who've been there two or even three years. All of them have been able to gain valuable experience in a City law firm, which will put them in very good stead for the future, whether they end up training and qualifying with us or elsewhere.'*

Legal executives

Legal executives work in many areas of law, frequently specialising in property matters and conveyancing, personal injury work, criminal and civil litigation, local authority work, corporate and commercial law, or the administrative side of legal practice.

Once certain qualifications are obtained from the Chartered Institute of Legal Executives (through a combination of legal work experience and exams – see Chapter 7), a legal executive is permitted to work in the areas of law covered by their qualification, allowing them to build up considerable expertise. They can do similar work to solicitors, often managing their own cases and matters, and may become leaders in their field. In private practice, legal executives may be fee earners, having their time billed to clients, thereby directly generating income for the firm. The main difference between a legal executive and a fully qualified solicitor (or barrister) is that they will not have gained the full range of experience required for formal qualification. This means there will be areas on which they will not be qualified to advise or work, or for which they or their employers might not be insured. In practice, a legal executive may do all the preparatory and practical work on a particular matter, with the work being reviewed and signed off by a partner, or other qualified lawyer. Otherwise, there can sometimes be little to differentiate an experienced legal executive from a fully qualified lawyer.

Specialist legal roles

Patent and trademark attorney

Patent agents are members of the Chartered Institute of Patent Attorneys who specialise in patent law. They advise clients as to whether rights can be obtained and protected in relation to an invention, and, if so, what the procedures will be, as well as advising on challenging or enforcing rights already in place. The technical and industrial nature of patent work is such that many employers view a science degree or other industrial experience as a distinct advantage, and since many registration systems are located outside the UK, a working knowledge of French, German or other languages can be useful.

Trademark attorneys are members of the Institute of Trade Mark Attorneys, and specialise in the law protecting the identity of a product or service. A trademark creates brand recognition and public confidence that the trademarked item is what it claims to be, and allows investment to be made in marketing the item. Trademarks are protected through a formal process, which gives the owner of the mark certain rights to prevent the mark being copied. Trademark attorneys advise on all aspects of trademark law, on the licensing of marks for use by parties other than the registrant, and on challenging or resisting a challenge to a registration, or potentially infringing use of a mark.

Licensed conveyancer

A licensed conveyancer is a lawyer with specific qualifications relating to property law, and who is entitled to act for a client when purchasing, selling or remortgaging property. Some licensed conveyancers are also qualified to provide probate services, as sale of property is a common element in dealing with a deceased person's estate. Several routes to qualification are available, which makes this area popular with people from any background. Once licensed, a conveyancer may work for an employer, either in private legal practice or in-house, or they may set up their own conveyancing practice. Licensing, regulation, education and monitoring of the profession are provided through the Council for Licensed Conveyancers.

Practice development lawyer/professional support lawyer

Practice development or support lawyers (PDLs or PSLs) often work in private practice law firms and give assistance to the firm, or departments within the firm, in a number of areas. These usually include researching and monitoring important developments in the law, managing legal training and professional development, writing articles and training materials, and assisting in practice management and business development. PDLs are usually qualified solicitors or barristers, but do not generally work on fee-earning matters, allowing them to focus on being expert consultants within their departments or firms, effectively acting as 'lawyers' lawyers'.

Costs lawyer

Costs incurred in contentious legal matters can be very significant, and, in more complex cases, can be incurred over a long period of time. Costs often make up a critical part of the terms of any legal settlement, and may be disputed after the substantive legal claims have been decided in a case. The general rule in litigation is that the loser of a claim pays the winner's costs, but in practice it is very unlikely that the winner will recover 100% of their costs from the loser, particularly if costs are disputed.

Costs lawyers are members of the Association of Costs Lawyers, and specialise in dealing with aspects of legal costs and cost-related litigation. They may be required to draft a detailed bill of costs incurred during a case, for review if disputed by the paying party. Fees due to a solicitor by a client may also be subject to dispute, and a costs lawyer may advise either party on the legal and procedural aspects to the recovery or payment of fees. Costs lawyers also advise on budget management, particularly when litigation or dispute resolution procedures are likely to be lengthy and expensive. The work of a costs lawyer is a unique combination of litigation practice and procedure, financial acumen and numeracy, and it can play as important a part in proceedings as that of a solicitor or barrister.

Notary

Notaries are qualified lawyers providing specialist services of authenticating and certifying documentation, usually for use abroad, and often in the context of diplomatic or immigration work. Advances in technology mean that many parts of the world do not require documentation to be officially certified, so the work is relatively specialised, with notaries often requiring knowledge of specific laws in specific territories in order to ensure that the correct procedure is followed. Notaries may also offer general legal services similar to solicitors, with the exception of litigation work, and are governed by similar rules of professional conduct to solicitors.

Legal support roles

It is rare for any legal practice to operate without the assistance of support staff, including librarians, legal secretaries and HR managers, many of whom hold legal qualifications as well as vocational qualifications relevant to their day-to-day role. More information on some of these roles is set out in Chapter 12.

How law firms and legal practices work

We have had a look at some of the key legal roles, so how do they work in practice? Solicitors and barristers work in different ways, so it is worth looking at each in turn.

Solicitors

As we have seen, solicitors usually work in partnerships or 'firms'. You will come across many different law firms of all shapes and sizes as your career progresses, but they can generally be broken down into a few main categories: full service firms, high-street firms, and niche firms.

Full service solicitors' firms

Full service law firms are divided into departments, each of which will deal with specific areas. There will be some crossover of work between the departments and teams of specialists, but the majority of work will be specific to each department. A large law firm may be divided into the following departments:

- antitrust/competition

- banking/finance/investments

- corporate

- employment

- insurance

- intellectual property

- litigation

- personal injury

- real estate/property/construction

- regulatory

- tax

- technology, media and telecommunications.

International firms and the large- or medium-sized City-based firms are often (but not always) structured this way, to reflect the nature of the work they tend to focus on.

High-street firms

High-street firms are usually much smaller than full service firms, and may focus less on areas of commercial law and more on matters relating to individuals. There is sometimes more crossover of work between departments, with individual lawyers taking on a broader range of matters. High-street firms may offer some commercial services to local businesses, but all will specialise in personal, day-to-day legal issues that affect people, such as buying and selling property, dealing with disputes, writing wills, planning trusts and tax, advising on family or divorce law and occasionally taking on criminal cases.

Niche firms

Specialist, 'niche' firms fall some way between the two. These often cater to a particular industry, which may require more specialist lawyers with deeper knowledge of their specific areas. Some are very small, being made up of only a few expert lawyers, while others can compete with equivalent departments at some of the larger firms, particularly in areas such as media and technology, employment or property law.

Barristers' sets

We saw earlier how most barristers have expertise in a few practice areas, often working in sets with complementary skills. Barristers' sets are often structured in such a way that the set as a whole offers a wide range of services through the combination of areas of expertise of the set's members. Some sets will offer more general legal and litigation services, while others offer services tailored towards more specialist areas such as family law, intellectual property, or construction and engineering law.

Alternative and new ways of working

The traditional way in which lawyers generate income is through being instructed or retained on matters that require their expertise, with clients paying an hourly or daily rate for each lawyer's time. The rate is agreed in advance, but the exact amount of time to be spent (and therefore the final bill) will vary on a case-by-case basis, as a matter progresses. The final fee will be known only at the end of the matter, once the work is done. Professional obligations of honesty and acting in a client's best interest are in place to prevent abuse of the system, but it is still far from perfect.

Today's clients demand greater visibility on how lawyers charge for their work, and demand greater flexibility of approach. The legal market has developed and a range of different types of law firm has appeared in response to these market demands. Regulation has also changed in recent years and has opened the legal world up to new business structures, which are altering the landscape of the profession in ways that will only become fully apparent in years to come.

Certain provisions of the Legal Services Act 2007 came into force in October 2011, permitting, among other things, law firms to seek external funding into their businesses, introducing external shareholders and investors into the legal profession. Traditional law firm partnerships or LLPs may no longer remain the predominant law firm structure. Instead, 'alternative business structures' (ABS) have been introduced, allowing non-legal companies such as banks or supermarkets to merge with legal providers. They are able to offer legal services in the same way as they offer other services not usually associated with their core business, and while it is too early to say whether ABS will ultimately prove to be a threat or an opportunity to the legal profession as a whole, it will certainly be interesting to see how the profession responds.

Some alternative legal business structures and organisations are given below, all of which operate in slightly different ways. In terms of employability, bear these organisations in mind, as they may offer additional opportunities, and more flexible ways of working than those offered in the more traditional legal practices.

Alternative legal structures

Co-operative legal services – the 'Co-op'

The UK's largest consumer cooperative has a long history and operates in many areas, including food shops, funeral services, insurance, banking, farming and travel services, with an emphasis on value and social responsibility. Its legal service extends the Co-operative brand and ethos, offering services that will be found in many high-street law firms: personal injury advice, employment advice, property and conveyancing, will writing and probate. Some contentious services are offered on a 'no win no fee' basis, while other services are billed at fixed rates for the work done.

Which? Legal Service

This is a legal service offered by the well-known consumer watchdog, Which? The service specialises in legal advice geared to individuals, as may be expected from its activities in other areas. The main services offered include advice on consumer rights, landlord and tenant issues, neighbour disputes, parking and clamping, and employment.

Clients pay for the service on a subscription basis, paying a monthly rate for unlimited contact with legal experts by phone and email, either during or out of office hours, depending on the level of subscription. Some self-contained areas of work are charged at a fixed fee.

Quality Solicitors

Quality Solicitors is an organisation looking to take advantage of looser regulation and increased opportunities for new business models through ABS to build a nationwide network of quality law firms operating under one recognised brand. Its aim is to offer consistently high-quality legal services through high-street practices that are already local market leaders. Local firms that meet the standards set by Quality Solicitors are recommended by the public and invited to join the Quality Solicitors network. Quality Solicitors operates through over a hundred branches across England and Wales, and has plans to expand further in the coming years.

Lawyers On Demand

This is a City-based, corporate and commercial legal service offered by law firm Berwin Leighton Paisner (BLP). A central group of qualified freelance lawyers are selected, trained and supported by BLP, to operate as a resource to be drawn on as and when the core resources of the firm need them. The use of freelancers reduces costs, while the support of a large City law firm guarantees the quality of services provided, and ensures that the best resources, training and support are in place for the freelance team. The service offers flexibility for clients and lawyers alike, as work may be allocated on the basis of a number of part-time hours per week for ongoing matters, while project-specific work may allow time to be apportioned on the basis of a number of full-time weeks or months.

Keystone Law

This is one of a number of solicitors' firms using technology to offer corporate and commercial legal services from a 'virtual' firm. Each solicitor works remotely from wherever they choose, sharing central law firm services. This structure can operate very efficiently, with cost savings being reflected in competitive rates. The downside for those early on in their career is that this particular firm's recruitment policy is to take on only experienced solicitors, preferably with an existing client base, so there is no opportunity to train with the firm.

New approaches to legal recruitment

Law Absolute

As the legal market has consolidated over recent years in response to recent economic conditions, there has been increased demand for part-time and interim lawyers, and a corresponding increased availability of lawyers looking to fill non-permanent vacancies. Law Absolute is a recruitment agency specialising in placing lawyers in temporary positions in private legal practice, and in-house in the commercial and public sectors. In addition to placing qualified and experienced solicitors and barristers, Law Absolute also has newly qualified lawyers, paralegals, legal assistants, contract managers and legal secretaries on its books, and is well worth bearing in mind when it comes to looking for legal work as your career progresses.

Summary

These alternative structures aim to offer improved legal services to the market, but their range and flexibility have the additional benefit of offering more diverse and flexible ways of working for lawyers at every stage of their careers. While there is no evidence to suggest that traditional ways of working will ultimately be replaced by these new entrants to the profession, the alternatives are certainly on the increase. This will make legal services more competitive on value and quality, and will also offer a broader range of career possibilities outside the traditional channels.

PART 3
Training and qualifying

6

The Academic Stage: getting the academic qualifications you need

In Chapter 1 we briefly looked at how the main stages of legal qualifications are divided, and how your career progression might evolve. In Chapters 4 and 5 we had a closer look at the main areas of law, and how work in legal practice relates to them.

In this chapter, we will look more closely at *how* you get the qualifications you need. Here we give you a brief guide to the main stages and requirements and a summary of the key stages of qualification, to help you navigate your way through. You should read this together with details given by specific course providers, and by the Solicitors Regulation Authority (SRA) or Bar Standards Board (BSB) – the organisations responsible for regulating the profession. Deadlines and procedures are likely to change from year to year, so make sure you check that the information you have is up to date.

Qualifications required to become a solicitor or barrister

Remind yourself of the stages of qualification on page 11. To recap, a law degree is usually the required entry-level qualification for all future lawyers, regardless of the area in which they wish to go on to specialise. This initial qualification can be gained either as a first undergraduate degree, or as a postgraduate 'conversion' course, i.e. the Graduate Diploma in Law (GDL). Both undergraduate and conversion law courses are recognised by the SRA and BSB and make up the 'Academic Stage' of qualification.

Once the Academic Stage is satisfied, the routes to qualification for future solicitors and barristers take different directions: this is the 'Vocational Stage'. To complete the Vocational Stage, solicitors are required to complete the Legal Practice Course (LPC), while barristers complete the Bar Professional Training Course (BPTC), formerly the Bar Vocational Course or BVC.

The Academic and Vocational stages are followed by professional training: either a solicitors' training contract, or barristers' pupillage.

Post-qualification: continuing professional development for solicitors and barristers

Practising solicitors and barristers are required to maintain their professional skills throughout their qualified career. There is a requirement to gain a certain number of continuing professional development (CPD) hours or 'points' throughout each year, according to each lawyer's level of experience. A proportion of each year's CPD points must come through participation in accredited courses or activities. The remainder can be made up from a wide range of other legally related activities, including teaching, writing articles, pro bono work or business development.

GCSEs and A levels

You may already have good grades at GCSE and A level, and an excellent academic record is the starting point for most legal careers, so it is important to be aiming high from the very start. Most course providers will not look at GCSE results, but some employers will, to assess the consistency of an applicant's CV. You may already have eight or more GCSEs – if they are all at grades A or B, this will usually be enough to satisfy most legal employers. At A level, the minimum that many firms and chambers will expect is two at grade A, and one at grade B.

If you do not have A levels, you should consider alternative qualifications, such as those offered by the CILEx. The CILEx Level 3 qualification is equivalent to A level Law, and serves as either a stand-alone introduction to law, or as the first stage of full qualification. See Chapter 7 for more information on CILEx options. Dealing with missing or problematic exam grades is discussed later in this chapter.

Looking to improve your tea-making and photocopying skills?

Apply elsewhere

Joining us for a week's placement or full Gap Year means getting fully involved. Working on real projects, alongside real life lawyers, learning about commercial law today, in the real world. We'll expect you to ask questions and have opinions. Ideas even. It may not be the experience that decides your career – but then again, it just might.

www.pinsentmasons.com/workexperience

Pinsent Masons

Profile: Pinsent Masons LLP

Our programmes

School work experience programme

We want to give ambitious candidates from any background the chance to experience life at a top law firm – demonstrating your proactive approach and developing your CV for university applications.

It doesn't matter which subjects you are studying, or which degree you plan to study. In fact, some 50% of our graduate trainees join us having completed a degree in a subject other than law. We do ask that you like solving problems, are 16 or over, well organised, smartly presented, bright, articulate, and willing to ask questions and get involved.

Over the placement you will also have the opportunity to listen to a number of presentations from trainee lawyers and qualified lawyers on what it is like to work at Pinsent Masons and why they decided to become commercial lawyers.

A student on the programme commented:

> *'Fantastic work experience. The programme was pitched just right and has cemented my desire to study law. Attending seminars, etc. and working alongside trainees was invaluable. I didn't just learn; I felt I added value.'*

Gap Year programme

Lasting eight months, our Gap Year programme offers solid, first-hand experience of commercial law before you start university. So if you're serious about a career in law, it's a chance to build a CV that will help you stand out from your peers.

Your typical duties will include drafting and proofreading documents and letters, carrying out research, liaising with clients by phone, email and face-to-face meetings, and getting involved in community work. We're looking for commitment, curiosity and enthusiasm, as well as good organisational skills, a smart appearance and the ability to think on your feet.

A former student commented:

> *'I received a warm welcome when I arrived in my department, which was employment. We were given a departmental induction and then it was straight into live work such as*

taking witness statements and drafting agreements. Over the year, I was involved in a confidential case, which involved attending court with the client, and I even got to write one of the monthly technical updates. It was great experience and I didn't realise how many doors it would open.'

How to apply

The placements are specifically for AS and A level students (or the equivalent) and school leavers. You can apply from 1 September via our website, where you can also find out more information (www.pinsentmasons.com/workexperience). The work experience programme typically has four intakes across the year and operates in all our UK offices. These are London, Birmingham, Leeds, Manchester, Edinburgh and Glasgow. The Gap Year programme operates in London, Birmingham and Leeds exclusively, but some students have relocated to undertake a placement as it is paid.

Law degree or conversion?

To complete the Academic Stage of training, you need to have completed either:

- a qualifying law degree

- a conversion law degree (GDL).

The Academic Stage of training requires both solicitors and barristers to have obtained the equivalent of a law degree at undergraduate level. The Academic Stage is overseen by a joint committee of the SRA and BSB, to ensure that qualifications comply with standards for both solicitors and barristers.

Qualifying law degrees

Most undergraduate law degrees are recognised as fulfilling the formal requirements of the Academic Stage of training, and are known as 'qualifying law degrees' because they reach the standards set by the SRA/BSB joint committee. You should check with your university to make sure that the law degree you have done, or are considering, will qualify.

Some course providers now offer two-year qualifying law degrees at LLB level. These are well worth considering, since this structure reduces the financial and time commitments of going through a full three-year degree. Bear in mind that there is one drawback: you will not be able to obtain vacation work or work experience in the summer break between years, as the course continues through the summer months. This may impact on your ability to gain valuable practical experience for your CV.

Entry requirements for a qualifying law degree

These are specified by each university or training institution (usually ABB at A level or equivalent).

Conversion degrees

If you do not hold a qualifying law degree, the Academic Stage of training can be satisfied by successfully completing a GDL 'conversion'. These courses take the key elements of the law degree and fit them into a one-year postgraduate course for those studying full-time, or into two years for part-time students. It's not always necessary to have an undergraduate degree to do a law conversion course.

Entry requirements for the GDL conversion degrees

For future solicitors, any of the following may be acceptable to satisfy the SRA requirements in order for an applicant to be eligible to go from the GDL to full qualification as a solicitor:

- undergraduate-level degree in any subject from a UK or Republic of Ireland university

- undergraduate-level degree in any subject from a non-UK university with an SRA Certificate of Academic Standing

- other degree-level qualification with an SRA Certificate of Academic Standing

- CILEx Level 3 and Level 6 qualifications.

For non-graduates, at least 10 years of academic, commercial or other professional or managerial experience is required, in order to be eligible for acceptance onto the GDL.

For future barristers, the BSB requires any one of the following for applicants to go from the GDL to full qualification as a barrister:

- UK honours degree at 2.ii level or above

- undergraduate-level degree in any subject from a non-UK university with a BSB Certificate of Academic Standing.

Non-graduates may also be accepted by the BSB Qualifications Committee on a case-by-case basis.

How to apply for the GDL

- Full-time course applications are *not* made direct to the course provider. All applications for full-time GDL courses must be made online via the Central Applications Board or CAB (www.lawcabs.ac.uk). A fee is required for applications to be processed.

- Applications for places on part-time courses, or courses taught through other study modes, are made direct to the course provider.

- In addition to your academic results and other details requested on the CAB form, you will need to provide references. These should be from academic tutors, where possible.

When to apply for the GDL

- The GDL usually starts in September each year. You will usually be given some pre-course materials a few weeks before the course starts, so it's important to get your application submitted in good time.

- Applications are accepted throughout the year via www.lawcabs.ac.uk. However, you should still aim to submit your application at least a few months before the course start date.

- You must enrol on the GDL (that is, actually start the course) no later than two weeks after the course enrolment date. This is to prevent you falling behind.

- Course dates are subject to change every year, so make sure you check the deadlines at www.lawcabs.ac.uk and/or with your course provider of choice.

- Contact your referees as early as you can, and make sure you allow plenty of time (at least a month) for them to respond.

Where to study the GDL

GDL and LPC courses are taught at institutions around the country, and the CAB website lists all eligible course providers, with links to their websites. This is the best place to start your research into where to study. Some are traditional universities, where it is possible to study law at undergraduate level, and then to go on to take the LPC. These universities include Birmingham, Cardiff, Nottingham and Westminster. Other course providers are more specialist, either providing professional/postgraduate training only, or legal training only. Some employers view these institutions as having the edge over their competitors, and it is true that some, such as The College of Law or BPP, have excellent reputations.

Note that the CAB system is purely an administrative service to manage applications for the GDL and LPC. CAB does not make any decisions as to who is allocated a place on which course.

Note also that while a qualifying law degree is valid indefinitely, those with a GDL qualification must go on to the LPC (or BPTC) within seven years; after that time the qualification expires.

The City Law School
CITY UNIVERSITY LONDON

World-class legal educ
in the heart of Lc

The best
legal
education
in towr

Undergraduate:
> LLB Law

Postgraduate:
> Graduate Entry LLB
> Graduate Diploma in Law
> LLM in EU Commercial Law
> LLM in International Banking
  and Finance
> LLM / M.Jur in International
  Commercial Law
> LLM in International
  Competition Law
> LLM in International
  Energy Litigation
> LLM in Maritime Law (UK)

> LLM in Maritime Law (Greece)
> LLM in Public International Law
> LLM in Criminal Litigation
> LLM in Civil Litigation and
  Dispute Resolution
> Masters in Innovation, Creativity
  and Leadership
> PhD, MPhil or LLM by Research

Professional:
> Legal Practice Course
> Bar Professional Training Course
> LLM in Professional Legal Practice
> LLM in Professional Legal Skills
> CPD courses

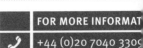

FOR MORE INFORMAT

+44 (0)20 7040 3309
www.city.ac.uk/law
law@city.ac.uk

When contacting us please quote the follo
reference: WL0912

Profile: The City Law School

A step in the right direction

Located in the heart of legal London, The City Law School provides legal training right where the law is being made. As one of the first major London law schools, it offers courses for every step of a student's legal career at undergraduate, postgraduate and professional level.

Based at Northampton Square in Clerkenwell and Gray's Inn in Holborn, the School offers the main professional courses for students aspiring to be solicitors or barristers: the Legal Practice Course (LPC) and the Bar Professional Training Course (BPTC).

City's LPC prepares students for professional life by offering a broad range of vocational subjects; these are taught to replicate the demands and disciplines of being in practice. For students still looking for a training contract, there's the School's Training Contract Advisory Service, which gives specialist career advice about getting that first foot in the door.

As the original provider of training for barristers, the School's BPTC is taught at master's level and gives students the knowledge to go on to a career at the Bar. The course also provides students with a range of transferable skills that can be used in a wide range of non-legal professions. Students are provided with their best chance of success at the Bar by having access to a dedicated Pupillage Advisory Service (PAS), which provides students with expert guidance about starting a career at the Bar.

For non-law graduates looking to start a legal career, the School offers the Graduate Diploma in Law (GDL) – a conversion course that allows students to transfer into law. Started in 1976, the GDL was one of the first conversion courses in the country and teaches students the seven core foundation modules from an undergraduate LLB in just one year.

All students can further bolster their professional connections by attending a range of events at the School where they can meet members of both sides of the profession. Dean of The City Law School, Susan Nash, explains: 'We have great links with the legal profession in London due to our locality and history, which enables us to provide huge levels of interaction between our students and the profession.'

City is at the forefront of modern legal education; students on all courses are given one-on-one support and encouraged to learn by doing in a real-life environment. Susan adds: 'This is a place where you can get personalised, life-long learning and, if you're genuine about law, we can offer you an education that is as much about life experience as it is about academia.'

With this many acclaimed courses and a modern approach to learning, The City Law School really is the school for professionals.

Case study

Leon Pickering attended The City Law School and completed his Graduate Diploma in Law in 2008/09 and his Bar Professional Training Course (then known as BVC) in 2009/10

About me

I'm originally from Norwich and I went to Oxford University, initially intending to be an academic. I studied Medieval English (MA, MPhil); however, friends of mine looked like they were having so much fun at the Bar that I jumped ship.

Why City

I found City's location to be absolutely unparalleled – it's inside one of the Inns of Court at Gray's Inn. Studying for the BPTC in the very environment where I was going to go on to practise cannot be beaten.

Teaching and support

The teaching at the School is excellent. Advocacy training is perhaps one of the most entertaining (and surreal) learning experiences I have ever had! Everyone was very interested in who I was and what I wanted to do: it didn't feel like a sausage factory. I found the School's personal tutor system very useful and there is a strong pastoral support network, too.

Benefits

The School has its own library at Gray's Inn Place, which is very well stocked with practitioner books. I also had access to the huge law library at the university's main campus at Northampton Square, which is equipped with just about every academic text you could need. Lawbore Pro is also an absolutely fantastic resource – very similar to that available at leading law firms and chambers.

Law in London

London is where the biggest and most exciting law cases happen. Living in London makes it so easy to go on mini-pupillages and vacation schemes – or even pop into the Royal Courts of Justice or the Old Bailey for a day. Nowhere else can match this.

Future career

Thanks to some great support and advice, I've been able to secure a pupillage at Ten Old Square. Following studying at City, I am confident that I will be able to hit the ground running.

What the GDL (or law degree) covers

The Academic Stage (i.e. law degree or GDL) covers the main areas of law that together make up the basis of all legal practice. We looked at the seven legal foundation subjects in Chapter 4, and these make up the majority of the course content.

Introductory course materials

You will usually be set some pre-course study materials before the GDL starts, including a course in legal method. This is taught and assessed early on in the GDL, well before the main foundation subject exams. Areas covered include an introduction to the English legal system, and interpretation and analysis of statutes and cases. These are areas that will crop up time and again throughout your legal career, so it is important to get a good grounding in the basics at an early stage. Some providers include an introduction to aspects of commercial law (for example general commercial practice and company law) at this point.

Core subjects

These are the foundation subjects of contract law, constitutional and administrative law, criminal law, equity and trusts, EU law, land law and tort law we covered on pages 49–54. The GDL covers these areas of law as separate academic subjects, setting out their background and development, and current status of the law in each area. In contrast to a traditional three-year law degree, the foundation subjects are all taught in parallel throughout the GDL, with each foundation course subject progressing simultaneously. For this reason, there are certain areas that only really link up towards the final stages of the GDL, and it can be very satisfying to have a 'eureka' moment, when things finally come together.

Generally, the GDL courses are taught as a combination of lectures and smaller study group sessions. There is usually the equivalent of one lecture per week per foundation subject, and perhaps three or four small group sessions. It is important to consolidate material covered in each lecture, to be ready for the next one, and it is essential to be properly prepared for each small group session. For these, you will be expected to have done preparatory reading, and to have prepared written exercises for discussion in class, as well as preparing and taking part in occasional group tasks. Time constraints mean that the courses are structured so that you absolutely must do the preparatory work for all classes. You will not pick up all the information you need for the exams unless you have covered the preparatory material for each and every class, and have done the follow-up work as the course progresses.

Coursework

The purpose of coursework is not so much to delve into a subject in detail, but rather to develop legal research skills. Two legal research assessments are generally set on the GDL. The first is a shorter written assignment which relates to one of the foundation subjects, with each student being allocated a particular question relating to an area of law. The second assessment is longer and more detailed, and usually takes the form of a dissertation or problem-based question, on an area of law that each student can choose according to their own interests.

Your link to the legal profession

We offer a full range of courses to prepare you for life as a legal practitioner.

LLB/GDL/LPC/BPTC/LLM/MSC/MBA

Flexible full-time, part-time and distance learning routes available

**To find out more call 0191 243 7035
or visit NorthumbriaLawSchool.co.uk**

northumbria
UNIVERSITY

School of Law

Profile: Northumbria Law School

Overview

Northumbria is justifiably renowned for excellence in learning and teaching and offers a ground-breaking portfolio of programmes at undergraduate, postgraduate and professional levels. We focus on law in practice and are committed to ensuring that our students develop the knowledge and skills needed to become successful legal professionals. This commitment is demonstrated through our academic staff, the majority of whom have considerable and often continuing experience of practice. We provide an extensive careers and employability programme and our graduates are highly sought after by employers both regionally and nationally.

Undergraduate programmes

Our innovative LLB (Hons)/M Law Exempting programme allows students to achieve a qualifying law degree, a master's and exemption from the Legal Practice Course. We are the only university in the UK to offer the LLB (Hons)/M Law Bar Exempting programme, an integrated master's degree incorporating the Bar Professional Training Course. For a small number of students there is also the possibility of following our LLB (Hons)/M Law Solicitor programme, a degree leading to full qualification as a solicitor.

The Law School offers a suite of Law+ programmes, a range of specialist law degrees including LLB (Hons) Law with Environment, LLB (Hons) Law with Property Management, LLB (Hons) Law with Business and LLB (Hons) Law with International Business.

Professional programmes

We are a leading provider of the Graduate Diploma in Law (GDL) for non-law graduates looking to practise law, the Legal Practice Course (LPC) for aspiring solicitors and the Bar Professional Training Course (BPTC) for aspiring barristers. Our students have the opportunity to gain a master's whilst studying the LPC or BPTC – a qualification which will undoubtedly benefit students when they embark upon their training contract or pupillage.

Postgraduate programmes

Northumbria has an enviable reputation for its practical, innovative master's programmes, which are accessible to a wide range of professionals. Various programmes can be studied on a full-time basis, although many students now opt to study via distance learning, which provides a flexible approach more suited to busy lifestyles. Our master's programmes include Child Law, Commercial Law, Employment Law and Medical Law to name but a few. An MSc in Business with Legal Management and an MBA in Legal Management are also available.

Location

The Law School is located on a modern, award-winning development in central Newcastle – City Campus East. Our students are taught in purpose-built accommodation which includes state-of-the-art lecture theatres, workshop rooms equipped with the latest technology and courtrooms modelled on those that students will experience as qualified practitioners.

The building also houses the School's internationally renowned Student Law Office, which provides our students with the opportunity to offer legal advice and representation to members of the public and thus experience life as a professional lawyer.

Contact us

For further information on the range of programmes offered by Northumbria Law School, please visit www.northumbrialawschool.co.uk, call 0191 243 7035 or email law@northumbria.ac.uk.

Case study

Victoria Smith is a GDL, LPC and LLM graduate

What was it about the course that particularly appealed?

I was really drawn to the fact that you can do a master's alongside the LPC. This is a great opportunity to get a further qualification. It has enabled me to develop my research skills and expand my knowledge of a particular area of law which will be useful in practice.

What do you like most about the course?

I really like the fact that the course is very practical. We learn skills such as interviewing, advocacy, legal writing and drafting. These are the type of skills that are essential to a career in law. I now feel that I can apply the knowledge that I gained during the Academic Stage of training. The LPC at Northumbria has thoroughly prepared me for starting work as a trainee solicitor.

How do you get on with your tutors and university staff?

The tutors and staff are very approachable and friendly on an academic and personal level. The open-door policy means you are encouraged to drop by any time you need to speak with a tutor or member of university staff. They provide great support both during and after the course has ended. I feel confident that I have had the best guidance possible to start my career. They have shown a great interest in my future, and are keen to keep up to date with my progress.

Why did you choose Northumbria?

I chose Northumbria because of its great location. I came to an open day before doing the GDL and stayed on to do the LPC. I have now spent two years studying at Northumbria and can confidently say that I made the right decision to study here.

What are you doing next?

I have secured a training contract with Dickinson Dees. When I start I know that I will have the support of Northumbria behind me.

How the GDL works in reality

The vast majority of the subject matter is assessed by exams at the end of the course. For full-time students, this means one three-hour paper for each of the seven subjects, usually sat one per day across a two-week period. Exams are usually a combination of essay questions and problem questions, designed to test your knowledge of the legal principles of each of the foundation subjects. More practical considerations, such as how a legal problem might perhaps affect a client in daily life, are not covered on the GDL, and are reserved for the LPC or BPTC. Generally, each exam counts as 10% of the overall GDL grade – 70% of your GDL is therefore exam-based, with only 30% available through coursework assessments.

The course contents of the GDL are similar to those of a full undergraduate law degree. The obvious advantage of fitting the course into the equivalent of one academic year is that it is possible to gain an initial legal qualification without having to make the financial and time commitment to law as a first degree. The disadvantages are that the GDL is very time pressured, and cannot offer the exposure over time to the various subjects you cover. If you go on to do the LPC or BPTC, you may feel that you have not had the time to properly absorb the subject matter to the same extent as those who have spent three years studying the same foundation subjects on law degrees.

The point about pressure is worth emphasising. The formal time requirement for the GDL is 32 weeks of tuition, with each week taking in 45 hours of lectures, tutorials and private study. Most GDL courses start in September, with exams usually scheduled the following June. This means that, in reality, all the teaching is squeezed into about nine months. All seven foundation subject exams are then sat in succession, usually one per day for four days in one week, followed by one exam per day for three days of the following week. When you add the coursework assessments and mock exams into the equation, you can see that these courses are quite intensive.

The GDL is intellectually and academically challenging, and the subject matter is very broad in scope. There is a lot of material to cover and to learn, and as we have seen, the vast majority is tested at the end by exams. You need to think carefully about whether this is right for you – most students manage the GDL well, albeit with some stressful times around exams and during some of the tougher course modules. However, the keys to success lie in being organised, focusing on the work you need to do, and being aware of the relatively short amount of time available to get on top of the subject matter. As one former GDL student puts it: 'Treat it like a full-time job – keep on top of things as you go through the course, and don't leave anything to the last minute. If you're not clear on something, speak to your tutors or classmates as soon as you can. That way you can't go wrong.'

Case study

David Swain is an associate solicitor at Simmons and Simmons, and studied for his GDL full-time

The GDL is a full-time commitment: you have lectures and classes all day, then you need to work in the evenings to catch up and prepare. You have to focus straight away, as you only have one year to get everything done. Everyone's in the same position, though, and discussions between people in your group are very interesting. The work is condensed, and doing seven core subjects simultaneously can feel a bit overwhelming at times, especially when you are doing subjects that would be taught in different years on an undergraduate law degree. You have a lot of fun, though, and it's generally easy to have a good work–life balance.

When it gets to exams it is quite intense, particularly as the exams are very close together. It's not like a modular degree course when different things are tested in different years. It is probably one of the more difficult sets of exams you can do, because even though the subjects fall under the umbrella of 'law', it is amazing how different they all are, with their own case law, statutes and so on.

Overall, managing the GDL workload gives you a good idea of what life in law is like, with tight deadlines, and working on several matters in parallel. You really get an understanding of how useful a network of friends and contacts can be. Bouncing ideas off each other, working as a team, working with people – these are essential skills for any lawyer.

Modes of study available

The details of conversion courses and modes of study differ between course providers, but they are generally offered in three varieties.

One-year full-time

The one-year full-time course requires attendance at lectures and small group classes throughout the week, from September to June, with short breaks for Christmas and Easter. As mentioned earlier, the GDL is usually made up of 32 weeks of teaching, with around 45 hours of classes and lectures per week, with additional time needed for preparation between classes, plus time for the introductory course and written assignments.

The full-time GDL packs a great amount of course and assessment work into the shortest possible time, but allows you to concentrate on it exclusively. Your teaching time will be spent with a group of fellow students whom you will see regularly throughout the year, giving you a support network that might prove invaluable when it comes to revising and preparing for assessments!

Two-year part-time

The two-year part-time courses require about 23 hours' attendance per week, split across study days that are held during the day, in the evening, or at the weekend. Again, preparatory work is required between classes, with the part-time courses being designed specifically for those with other commitments. The seven foundation subject exams are done at the end of each of the two years, with exams in four subjects at the end of the first year, and the remaining three at the end of the second year.

Mixed

Some institutions offer the option to study the GDL over 18 months. Subjects are taught through a combination of online tutorials and attendance at a small number of study days (fewer than 10 in total) across the year, with supervision available as needed by individual students.

Part-time or full-time?

The general view is that the full-time GDL offers the highest amount of face-to-face contact with tutors and fellow students, and has the advantage of allowing the qualification to be obtained in the shortest possible amount of time. It is commonly accepted that balancing work, family or other commitments makes it harder for part-time students to focus on their academic work. When choosing a GDL provider, look out for those that offer a high ratio of tutor-to-student contact, a high ratio of lectures to small group classes, and those that can offer some flexibility through the use of online resources. Part-time courses are popular and have good pass rates; it is possible to combine GDL study with other commitments, and to do well. Also, some providers include all course books and materials in the course fee, while others do not. Shop around, and be sure to look carefully at what each course provider offers, and how their courses are taught and assessed, to make sure your GDL provider is the best fit for you.

Overcoming problem areas in academic qualifications

You can see that the application system for courses and training positions across the legal profession is very heavily focused on academic grades. The general requirements for most employers will be A grades at A level and GCSE, at least a 2.i in your degree, and at least a commendation on the GDL and/or LPC, or 'very competent' on the BPTC.

How earlier exam grades relate to legal practice

Many legal employers will require you to fill in an online application form, which will not let you progress unless you have submitted a number of UCAS points, usually equivalent to grades AAB at A level. If you have to apply through one of these sites, then the reality of the situation is that there is no way around this if you do not have the required grades. Unfortunately, you do not meet their eligibility criteria. However, this is not to say that there are no potential employers out there for you. Work on getting the best possible law grades you can, and combine these with legal work experience; you will find that this will help outweigh lower grades from life before law. There are many excellent legal employers out there who may not have the marketing budgets of the big firms you've heard of, but who are no less capable of offering fantastic training and employment opportunities. Keep up your research and contacts, and keep your eyes open, as there are plenty of opportunities out there.

Course providers will be less concerned at the odd lower grade on your CV, although you should still check eligibility criteria with the college or university where you intend to study, to make sure you have what is required. Course providers are happy to discuss this with prospective candidates. Contact them if you are in any doubt, or discuss any questions or concerns you have with representatives of the course providers at a course open day.

In reality, a lot of people experience the occasional blip in their academic career, and you might feel as though your grades, while generally good, do not tell the whole story, or that some lower grades reduce the overall quality of your academic record. If this is the case, then there are plenty of ways to go about addressing the issue, and ensuring your academic capabilities are seen in the most positive light. The following sections cover some of the most common issues, and ways they can be remedied.

Inconsistent grades at GCSE and/or A level

It is quite common for people to have a spread of grades, particularly when sitting a lot of exams in different subjects at the same time. Of course, your grades should indicate that you have the aptitude for law, and this may be shown by top grades in at least a few subjects. If your grades are good in some areas, but poor in others, then you should think about why this happened. Are there any reasons which properly explain why you did better in some subjects than in others? Can you work on this to prevent similar erratic results in the future? Remember that a career in law requires hard work, focus, concentration and stamina (as well as a lot of exams!), so you may need to look at how you approached the exams in which you did not do so well. Ask yourself if you would do things differently now, and, if so, how? Even if your previous grades are not great, the clearest and best way to demonstrate to an employer that you have what it takes for law is to do well in your law exams and assessments. This is entirely within your control, and with hard work and dedication, you will be able to get some very strong grades.

No A levels

For any number of reasons, either you may have decided not to do A levels, or you may have chosen a career path that did not require you to do them, if perhaps some other experience or qualification was required. This is not a barrier to entry to law, as there are qualification systems available to allow you to bridge these gaps. In particular, CILEx provides a range of options to gain equivalent qualifications, which are recognised by legal course providers and employers. Legal executive work is some of the best legal work experience there is, and this can be used to replace A levels, and to count directly towards qualification. Useful information and advice on routes to qualification for those without 'traditional' academic qualifications are available from CILEx (see page 124).

Again, your emphasis should be on getting the best grades you can in your legal studies, and to focus on getting good legal work experience. Many solicitors have come to law with no A levels, and have gone on to train, qualify and have very successful careers. It is possible to replace a set of exam grades you might have missed out on years ago with alternative legal qualifications. When combined with good, practical legal work experience, this can be a very attractive offering to an employer.

Mitigating circumstances

Legal employers do take mitigating circumstances into account, if these have been indicated by an applicant. It is worth bearing this in mind because all legal employers receive a high number of high-quality applications, and it would be perfectly possible for them to fill vacancies with the very best candidates, without even looking at people whose lower grades may be explained by perfectly valid reasons.

The important thing to remember is that an employer will only view as mitigating circumstances those situations that would genuinely prevent someone from performing to their optimum level through no fault of their own. This can't be used as a way to excuse poor performance because you had decided to concentrate on something other than your work, no matter how positive that other activity was. If you had a choice as to how you spent your time, this is unlikely to be considered a 'mitigating circumstance'. However, there are no hard and fast rules as to what 'counts', and you don't have to have been personally incapacitated. If, for example, a parent or other close family member was seriously ill or undergoing treatment while you were at university, then this may quite reasonably have prevented you from fully reaching your potential during your degree.

If you find yourself in this situation, then it is useful to include with your application a reference or explanatory statement from someone (preferably in a position of responsibility) who knew you at the time, as this will add credibility to your explanation. If you have any doubts as to how best to present this on a CV or application, you should speak to your careers adviser.

Not getting a 2.i or above in your first degree

If you were not awarded at 2.i or a First in your degree, then this will not generally prevent you from getting a place on the various law courses offered by most providers. Note, however, that the BSB requires at least a 2.ii before the GDL or BPTC in order for you to go on to qualify as a barrister. In any event, you should check each course provider's entry requirements before you apply. Use the CAB and BSB websites as a starting point.

Employers (law firms, sets of chambers, etc.) are inclined towards offering places to candidates at the higher end of the degree range. Like any employer, this is part of their remit to find the best people. Measuring candidates by academic results is a relatively consistent method of reducing the risk of taking on people who might not be suitable for the role, but this can be a relatively rough and ready benchmark of aptitude. Legal training positions invariably require more than just academic ability; grades alone may not reveal the full picture of an applicant's suitability.

However, sometimes the requirement to have a 2.i is not always a hard and fast rule. Sometimes a candidate with a lower degree, but very good additional attributes on their CV, may trump another applicant with little to offer other than good grades. Once again, you need to make sure that your CV is continually being improved, adding work placements or vacation schemes, and achievements in other activities as you acquire them. A strong, updated CV demonstrates that your motivation and dedication count for more than one or two weak spots on the academic side. If mitigating circumstances applied to you, then say so. Otherwise, focus on building up your CV through good legal grades and relevant work experience. This will show your overall achievements in a more positive light than your previous academic grades may suggest.

Summary

Academic results are important in law, and you need to work hard to get the best grades possible in your law exams. These are directly relevant to your career, much more so than a bad GCSE grade in an unrelated subject years ago. Aim high: try to get distinctions in all modules throughout your GDL, LPC and/or BPTC, and if you put the work in, you will do very well in at least some – if not all – areas. If your better grades match the areas of law you are interested in, then so much the better. This will make it much easier to sell yourself to firms or sets of chambers that may work in these areas. If you did well in areas you do not expect to practise in, keep an open mind. If your grades indicate strengths in areas of law you had not previously considered, then this may suggest a relevant aptitude for these areas; and perhaps you should investigate career possibilities in these areas. You may well find that opportunities come along as your contact with legal work continues, and in areas of law that you had not considered before.

When you have acquired your qualifying law degree or conversion, you have satisfied the Academic Stage of training, and are eligible to go on to the Vocational Stage of training for either solicitors or barristers.

7

The Vocational Stage of training

As we mentioned earlier (and see page 11), once the Academic Stage is completed, the training for solicitors and that for barristers takes separate routes, specific to the skills required for each profession. We will look at each in turn, starting with the vocational training required for solicitors.

The LPC for solicitors

Before starting a training contract, all future solicitors must complete the Legal Practice Course (LPC). The LPC is the springboard for taking the theoretical law you have learned in the foundation subjects at the Academic Stage, and applying this to everyday legal situations that practising solicitors face in their working life.

The course contents are prescribed by the Solicitors Regulation Authority (SRA), with an emphasis on the practical application of the law to client-specific cases, and learning to advise clients appropriately. This is a move away from identifying and analysing points of law in isolation, as tends to be the case at the Academic Stage.

Objective

To complete the solicitors' Vocational Stage of training, you will need to have:

- completed the LPC

- enrolled with the SRA, with confirmation of completion of the Academic Stage of training.

LPC entry requirements

- Completion of the Academic Stage of training (through qualifying law degree or conversion, as above, or confirmation from the SRA that an overseas equivalent qualification is acceptable).

- Enrolment with the SRA as a student member.

- Written confirmation of completion of the Academic Stage of training from the SRA.

How to apply for the LPC

- As with the Graduate Diploma in Law (GDL), *all* applications for full-time LPC courses must be made online via the Central Applications Board (CAB; www.lawcabs.ac.uk). A fee is required for applications to be processed.

- Applications for places on part-time or alternative study mode LPC courses should be made direct to the course provider.

- There is no obligation to study the GDL and LPC at the same college or university, if both courses are offered. Many providers of both courses will offer guaranteed LPC places to their GDL students, as well as assistance in the application process. There are advantages to studying both GDL and LPC at the same place, and other advantages to changing course provider – the choice is yours.

When to apply for the LPC

- The LPC usually starts in September of each year, although alternative LPC structures may start earlier.

- Course dates are subject to change every year, so make sure you check the deadlines at www.lawcabs.ac.uk and/or with your course provider of choice.

Where to study the LPC

As with the GDL, institutions offering the LPC are listed on the CAB website. These are similar to those offering the GDL, and fall into the same categories of 'traditional' universities, or more specific professional or postgraduate training providers. The same considerations apply when selecting where to study the LPC as we looked at for the GDL on page 91.

How to enrol as a student member of the SRA, and obtain confirmation of completion of your Academic Stage of training

- Use the SRA's online registration system to apply for both enrolment and confirmation of the Academic Stage (www.sra.org.uk/students/student-enrolment.page). A fee is payable.

- Applications should be submitted to the SRA one month before the start of the LPC.

- Your Academic Stage course results should be submitted to the SRA two months after the start of the LPC at the latest, or within one month for students on shorter LPC courses. Your LPC course provider can help you with this.

- Note that the application for enrolment requires a declaration that you are of a suitable character to join the profession. All applicants are asked to provide information on convictions, bankruptcies, county court judgments, acts of plagiarism, and other investigations to which they may have been subject, and to give information on anything else that might call their suitability into question.

- Note also that it is your responsibility to ensure you have enrolled with the SRA and obtained confirmation of completion of the Academic

> Stage. The SRA no longer sends reminders to potential LPC students, as in previous years.

When you have completed your solicitors' Vocational Stage of training, you are eligible to start your professional training, as a trainee solicitor.

LPC course content

The LPC is split into two parts: the compulsory stage and the elective stage. The compulsories are covered in the first few months of the LPC, with exams in late spring. The elective modules and exams take place in the summer.

There are additional compulsory assessments along the way, which take various forms, including legal research, interviewing clients, preparing simple accounts and face-to-face advocacy. We will look at those in a moment.

> There are more than 15 exams and assessments in all throughout the LPC, with additional mock exams and assessments available to help you, so bear in mind that you need to pace yourself as the LPC progresses!

Compulsory stage

The compulsory stage is made up of the areas that every solicitor is required to have covered, as prescribed by the SRA. These are split into the following four areas:

1. LPC core subjects:
   - business law and practice
   - litigation (civil and criminal)
   - property.
2. course skills
3. professional skills
4. elective subjects.

LPC core subjects

Business law and practice

This is important for all solicitors, regardless of the area of practice you end up in. The majority of clients you will come across will operate in a commercial context of one sort of another, and even if you decide to work in a less commercially focused area, such as criminal or family law, you will need to know how to run your own practice. This element of the LPC is designed to give you the insight you need into many of the issues affecting commercial enterprises, whether or not you will advise on them in a professional capacity later in your career.

The main areas covered in this module are the following.

- Partnerships: formation and dissolution of partnerships, terms of agreement and liability.

- Companies: formation and management, shareholders' rights, directors' duties, funding and capital structures.

- Corporate security and insolvency: types of security, administration and receivership, company voluntary arrangements, liquidation, personal bankruptcy, disqualification of directors.

- Business relationships: employment, commercial contracts, trading relationships.

- Taxation: income tax, inheritance tax, capital gains tax, corporation tax, value added tax (VAT).

- Business accounts: book-keeping, profit and loss accounts and balance sheets for sole traders, partnerships and companies, year-end adjustments and interpretation of accounts.

Litigation – civil

Solicitors working in all practice areas are required to have a good working knowledge of both civil and criminal litigation. Clearly this is crucial for those choosing to specialise in contentious work, but litigation can occur in any number of different contexts, and all solicitors should have a good understanding of how litigation works in practice, and what the procedures and considerations are in the context of legal disputes.

The civil litigation compulsory module covers high court and county court litigation under the Civil Procedure Rules (CPRs, published in the *White Book*). The course covers important aspects of court procedure and the key skills required in the civil litigation process:

- pre-action considerations

- commencement proceedings

- interim matters

- evidence

- strategy and tactics

- trial and enforcement costs and funding

- jurisdiction

- non-litigation/alternative dispute resolution.

Criminal Litigation

This module is an introduction to the skills needed by solicitors involved in criminal work, and covers the procedures at all stages of a criminal case, from initial arrest of the suspect to disposal of the case. The course is usually taught around a series of scenario-based case studies.

Elements covered on the course include:

- advising the suspect at the police station

- detention, and dealing with the custody officer

- applying for legal aid

- bail applications

- where the case will be heard (magistrates' court, Crown court, or other court)

- assessing the cases of the prosecution and defence, and managing evidence

- sentencing

- professional conduct rules affecting criminal practice and advocacy

- human rights law, and the effect of the European Convention on Human Rights and Human Rights Act 1998 on aspects of criminal litigation.

In both civil and criminal litigation modules, you will find that the legal issues are not particularly complex or hard to identify, to the same extent they might have been at the Academic Stage. Instead, the emphasis at LPC level is on the wider issues around a case or claim, introducing you to more practical matters that a solicitor will deal with, over and above the 'black letter' law.

Property law and practice

Having covered the legal foundations of land law on your law degree or conversion course, the purpose of the LPC property module is to set the legal theories in the context of practical conveyancing, and the solicitor's role in buying and selling property. It provides very useful grounding for solicitors wishing to specialise in property work, but is useful for all solicitors, since many commercial transactions include a property element. Even if property law is likely to play a minor role in your qualified career, an understanding of the conveyancing process is useful in your life outside work, when buying, selling or renting your own property.

The main areas covered on the property law and practice module are:

- introduction to the conveyancing process, and the legal and practical skills required

- drafting contracts and transfers of property

- searches and enquiries

- e-conveyancing

- standard conditions of sale, and standard commercial property conditions

- problem areas such as the creation of new easements, covenants, new and existing mortgages

- commercial leases

- planning law

- VAT on property transfers

- financing property transfers

- the role of other professionals in the conveyancing process

- drafting leases

- introduction to the Landlord and Tenant Act 1954 Part 2

- professional conduct considerations in the conveyancing process

- residential transactions: SRA protocol and documents.

Course skills

The LPC core subjects mentioned above deal with the practice areas that most solicitors work within, although not all solicitors will be involved with all three areas all of the time. By contrast, the 'course skills' are taught as separate course elements, and introduce you to skills and considerations that every solicitor needs, in all areas of practice.

Advocacy

While 'courtroom' advocacy is more generally associated with the work of barristers, it is common for solicitors (particularly those specialising in litigation) to be required to make applications before a judge, to represent clients in tribunals, and to act as an advocate in other contexts. On the LPC, advocacy techniques are taught in tutorials, with the assessments taking the form of a mock application before a judge.

You will either represent the claimant or respondent in a case, and will be expected to argue your case in front of a tutor or actor playing the part of the judge. A fellow student will represent the opposing party, and argue against you. The adversarial nature of the process might suggest that your performance is assessed on whether or not you successfully 'win' your application. In fact, what counts is demonstrating that you have researched your area well and have put forward a convincing legal argument, and that you respond to, and question, your opponent's points convincingly.

Interviewing and advising

This is again taught in class, where you are given the opportunity to practise interviewing techniques with your colleagues, while the assessments take the form of a scenario prepared in advance. You are required to interview an actor or tutor playing the part of the client, and to provide on-the-spot legal advice to them, in the context of the information they have given you in the interview.

If you feel that face-to-face assessments are not your strongest area, then take advantage of any practice interview opportunities available from your course provider. These are sometimes video-recorded, so you can see how you come across to your client – you may be surprised at what you see, and it can be very easy to spot areas for improvement, which can be a great help in approaching the assessments.

Drafting

A sizeable proportion of any solicitor's workload is taken up with drafting documents of one form or another. These might include legal agreements, court documents, written summaries of legal research and analysis, articles, policy guidelines or any number of other written pieces. For the LPC drafting assessment, you will be given a case study which requires a legal document to be produced.

Again, the legal issues are not particularly difficult to identify or understand at this stage; the scenario may perhaps require drafting a simple licence to occupy land for a specified period of time, or may be a detailed letter of advice to a client. What matters is to ensure that your drafting is well structured and succinct, using clear and unambiguous language, yet covers everything that the scenario requires.

Practical legal research

Good legal research skills are essential for all trainees, paralegals and qualified solicitors. Getting to grips with the array of legal resources available is something you need to master early on. Hard copy and online resources are both commonly used in practice, but have respective advantages and disadvantages, depending on the legal issue you are looking into. This element of the LPC covers both types of resource, with the emphasis on learning to navigate your way through them, and to present clear, concise written summaries of your results.

A note on accounts and advocacy

It may seem strange that would-be solicitors are required to study areas more commonly associated with accountants and barristers, but these are core skills that will stand you in good stead wherever you end up in your legal career. When it comes to advocacy, all solicitors find that the advocacy modules provide good training for speaking and thinking on your feet, and are good preparation for life beyond qualification.

Solicitors also find that having some experience in accounts is handy later on in the training process and beyond. A good handle on financial reporting is useful in any area of law, so there is good reason for accounts modules to be included in the LPC. Accounts assessments are not widely acknowledged as a student favourite, but they are pass/fail assessments whose individual marks do not count towards the overall LPC grade. Most candidates pass them first time, but if you need to retake either of the accounts exams (or other assessments), this is possible. Bear in mind that this may affect your ability to gain a commendation or distinction overall, regardless of whether you have attained the required marks to do so in other exams or assessments.

Case study

Daniel Turnbull is a partner at Stewarts Law LLP

I found the LPC quite straightforward, as I had worked in law for a long time before starting it. I had good background knowledge of some of the areas covered, and could easily place them in context. I liked the structured approach to the modules, and found it useful overall. The LPC teaches you to be structured in your thinking, and focused in your work, particularly in terms of how you prepare for exams.

Another thing the LPC teaches you is that you have to be prepared to put the work in. You can't just cram at the last minute, then turn up to the exams, and pass with good grades. The way the courses and the exams are put together means that you have to put the hours in. But if you do, it shouldn't be too difficult.

Other professional subjects

In addition to the course skills, a number of professional and regulatory areas are also covered on the LPC, as they affect many aspects of a solicitor's work.

Professional conduct and regulation

The SRA monitors the training and qualification of solicitors, and implements rules and regulations that govern the solicitors' profession as a whole. The SRA Code of Conduct 2011 is the foundation of the new 'outcomes-focused' regulatory system in which solicitors operate in England and Wales.

The code is based on 10 mandatory principles.

'You must:

1. uphold the rule of law and the proper administration of justice;

2. act with integrity;

3. not allow your independence to be compromised;

4. act in the best interests of each client;

5. provide a proper standard of service to your clients;

6. behave in a way that maintains the trust the public places in you and in the provision of legal services;

7. comply with your legal and regulatory obligations and deal with your regulators and ombudsmen in an open, timely and cooperative manner;

8. run your business or carry out your role in the business effectively and in accordance with proper governance and sound financial and risk management principles;

9. run your business or carry out your role in the business in a way that encourages equality of opportunity and respect for diversity; and

10. protect client money and assets.'[6]

The Code covers a wide range of potentially problematic areas that solicitors may face, such as conflicts of interest, confidentiality, referrals of business, publicity and issues specific to litigation work or selling property. The key elements of the Code are covered during the LPC, and issues of professional conduct can appear in any context in the course.

Another key area covered on this part of the LPC is financial regulation. Financial services and money-laundering regulations (particularly the Financial Services and Markets Act 2000, or FSMA) have had a big impact on the profession, and the LPC introduces you to the main financial and regulatory issues that solicitors are likely to face. Solicitors' accounts are also taught and assessed as part of the professional conduct element of the LPC. This is assessed by an exam, which is usually sat relatively early on in the LPC year.

Wills and administration of estates

A number of issues, both legal and practical, will occur when dealing with ownership of property of a person who has died. These will differ according to whether or not there is a properly executed will in place. This LPC module introduces each stage of the estate administration process, from initial representation of the client to distribution of assets of the estate to beneficiaries and the final winding up of the estate.

Compulsories: summary

The purpose of the compulsory stage of the LPC is to ensure that every solicitor is equipped with the core competencies required for a career in practice, no matter in which area you ultimately choose to specialise. The SRA approves individual teaching institutions on the basis that the required subjects are covered, and while there is some variance among institutions as to how the LPC is structured, the course content is very similar wherever you choose to study. Even though the course content may be similar, you should still do your research before you select an LPC provider, to check how the course is structured and see what else is on offer.

LPC elective stage

Once you have completed the compulsory stage of the LPC, you will go on to choose three further subjects from a number of different options ('electives').

The elective courses on offer will differ from one course provider to another, but the most common electives to be offered by most providers are:

- advanced commercial litigation/dispute resolution

- advanced commercial property

- banking and debt finance

- commercial law and intellectual property

- corporate acquisitions

- corporate finance

- employment law and practice

- family law

- insurance law

- welfare and immigration law

- personal injury and clinical negligence

- private clients

- public companies and equity finance.

By the time you come to choose your LPC electives, you will probably have a relatively good idea of which areas of law appeal to you the most, and where you are most likely to want to work. The electives offer the opportunity to fine-tune your learning to fit these areas, as a first step in adopting specialist legal knowledge. The elective subjects often match departments within some law firms, and when you come to do your training contract, you will find that the course contents fit very well with the day-to-day work done in those departments. Course providers ensure that all course contents are kept up to date every year, so you will find that your notes and resources will be invaluable when you make the transition from studying to practising as a trainee solicitor.

If you have a training contract in place by the time you choose your electives, then it makes sense to choose electives that match the work you will do with your firm.

If you are yet to secure a training contract, then it is important to choose a set of electives that does not limit your future options. Specific electives to choose will depend on individual circumstances, but if you see yourself in any commercial firm, for example, then any of the litigation- and finance-focused options will be useful. Areas such as employment, family, personal injury and private client law are not practice areas covered by all firms, and may sit better with general practice or high-street firms. Choose options that build your knowledge in your areas of interest, but be aware that narrowing your options at this stage may make your CV less appropriate for a broader range of potential firms to train with.

A note on LPC electives, from a City solicitor

'Your choice of electives is important, and this can influence where you can apply to train. Some firms will require you to do certain electives: pretty much all the big international and City firms will require you to do a corporate/commercial elective, a banking/debt finance elective, and public companies and/or acquisitions. These firms expect you to do these options because these areas are core to their business. This in turn serves as a big clue as to what to expect from these firms, if and when you train there. At other firms the options are not set in stone, but it might be harder to convince a firm that you are the right choice to offer a training contract if you have not chosen electives that coincide with that firm's main areas of work.'

Full-time or part-time?

The LPC can be studied as a one-year full-time course, requiring around 40 hours of study time per week, including attendance at a number of seminar-style classes, plus attendance at lectures and/or viewing online video tutorials, which are becoming increasingly popular.

Part-time courses are also available. These usually span two years, and require around 20 hours of study time per week. Additional time is required for attendance at exams, assessments and assessment practice. As with the part-time conversion courses, part-time LPC courses are intended to offer flexibility, and are a good way to gain your qualification while managing other commitments.

Case study

Ed Chivers is a solicitor at Farrer & Co, London

I did the GDL and the LPC. For me, the GDL was a return to academic education after a gap of a couple of years and I enjoyed it very much. It was both intellectually demanding and satisfying. As it was based around the theory of law rather than the practice of it, it suited my background well. I enjoyed the structure and the teaching, with discussion and debate built into it as a requirement of the course.

On the other hand, the LPC I did not enjoy so much, and I don't believe I learned as much that has really helped me in my qualified career as I did on the GDL. However, there is flexibility in the system, particularly as to whether or not you do the 'right' electives. By way of example, I now specialise in an area of law that I did not study at all on the LPC, and did not do as an elective. This has not been a problem, because it is only through working in law that you really learn about law and practice.

Case study

David Swain is an associate solicitor at Simmons and Simmons

The LPC is not very 'academic' as it is more about process and procedure of areas that all solicitors have to cover. Some people find it less interesting than their law degree or conversion for that reason. The LPC builds on your understanding of areas of law you might want to work in, but you should bear in mind at this stage that what you learn procedurally on the LPC is not exactly how things work in practice. In litigation, for example, the LPC course sets out deadlines and procedures involved in taking a court action all the way from start to finish. In reality, the timescales in litigation can be very long, so it is unlikely that as a trainee you will see a case all the way through. This will probably not happen until you have qualified, and have been working in a litigation department for perhaps a few years.

Because you are in a classroom, some areas of the LPC give a misleading impression of the work in real life, and do not show you how interesting or exciting some of the work can be. For example, it is only when as a trainee you go to the opponents' offices and serve a form on them, or when you go to the Royal Courts of Justice with a claim form and fee to commence a serious action that you realise that you are playing a part in something really major.

At times the LPC may not seem very interesting, or it may be hard to grasp the applicability of what you are covering, but it is a mandatory step, and without it you would be lost as a trainee. You need to have covered the main areas that later become relatively simple tasks, like legal research, knowing the sources of law, doing company searches, finding the right forms and filling them in correctly, or knowing the structure of the court system. You learn some of these things at law degree level, and they come into more context on the LPC, but they become fundamental once you start training.

Qualifications offered by the Chartered Institute of Legal Executives

The Chartered Institute of Legal Executives (CILEx) system is made up of a combination of academic qualifications and legal work experience that together lead to the qualification of legal executive. This is a professional qualification in its own right, alongside the qualifications of solicitor and barrister. CILEx lawyers can become partners in law firms, advocates and judges. With the appropriate CILEx qualifications and legal work experience, and subject to approval by the SRA, it is possible to use the CILEx route to qualify as a solicitor without having to complete a formal training contract in a law firm. However, many CILEx lawyers choose not to take the route to qualification as a solicitor, as their CILEx qualifications offer them everything they need, particularly given the vocational, practical aspects of the CILEx system. Most CILEx courses are taught part-time, and are designed for those already in work. You can choose to study at one of the 90 nationwide CILEx study centres, or by distance learning.

Academic requirements for CILEx

The recommended entry requirement for CILEx qualification is four GCSEs at grade C or above. If you hold no formal qualifications, these can be gained through introductory-level CILEx courses. CILEx places emphasis on diversity, and broadening access to the legal profession – you do not need to have a degree to obtain CILEx qualifications, and indeed many CILEx members see the route as an alternative to university.

If you have no law degree or equivalent, there are two CILEx qualifications available instead. The two qualifications required to become a legal executive are the CILEx

Level 3 Professional Diploma in Law and Practice, and the Level 6 Professional Higher Diploma in Law and Practice. The Professional Diploma is set at A-level standard, while the Professional Higher Diploma is set at degree level. These can be studied part-time or full-time, and should each take two years to complete. These qualifications allow you to become a graduate member of CILEx.

If you have a law degree or equivalent (such as a GDL), the CILEx Graduate Fast-Track Diploma serves as the equivalent to the LPC or BPTC.

Completion of the relevant CILEx qualification, together with a prescribed five years of practical legal work experience, allows you to become a qualified legal executive.

CILEx offers a broad range of legal qualifications in addition to those mentioned above, from legal secretarial qualifications for administrators to advocacy and court work qualifications for qualified lawyers. Further details on CILEx courses are available at www.cilex.org.uk.

The BPTC for barristers

Objective

To complete the barristers' Vocational Stage of training, you will need to have (in order):

- become a student member of an Inn of Court

- completed the Bar Professional Training Course (BPTC)

- been called to the Bar.

How and when to apply for student membership of an Inn of Court

- There are four Inns of Court – Gray's Inn, Lincoln's Inn, Inner Temple and Middle Temple (see Chapter 5 for more details). Applications for membership should be made direct to the Inn of your choice, through its online application form.

- Applications must be submitted by the end of May of the year in which you are due to start the BPTC.

BPTC entry requirements

- Completion of the Academic Stage of training: this is achieved either through obtaining a qualifying law degree or conversion at a minimum of 2.ii or equivalent (or confirmation from the Bar Standards Board (BSB) that an overseas equivalent qualification is acceptable).

- Membership of an Inn of Court: you are unable to start the BPTC without membership of an Inn (see above).

- Note that the BSB intends to introduce a pre-BPTC aptitude test in autumn 2012 to filter applicants for places on the BPTC (see box on page 127 for details).

How to apply for the BPTC

All applications for BPTC courses (full-time and part-time) must be made online via the BSB's central applications system (www.barprofessionaltraining.org.uk). A fee is required for applications to be processed.

When to apply for the BPTC

- The BPTC usually starts in September of each year.

- You should aim to complete your application as early as possible. The system opens mid-October of the year before the BPTC start date.

- The deadline for applications for the first round of BPTC selections is mid-January of the year the BPTC is due to start, with offers made in early March.

- Applications received after mid-January of the BPTC year are processed in a second round of selections, closing at the end of August. First-round offers must be accepted by early April, after which a clearing system operates to match candidates to potential places in time for the September start.

Eligibility for call to the Bar

- You need to have passed the BPTC before you can be called to the Bar (i.e. formal admission to the profession, through an Inn of Court).

- You need to attend 12 'qualifying sessions' at your Inn either during, or just after, your BPTC. These range from mooting and debating sessions to talks on legal subjects, and include dinners, drinks receptions and other social occasions.

- You need to submit a number of application forms to your Inn, known as 'call papers'. These are available from your Inn.

- All barristers are required to attend a formal call ceremony. These take place on four dates across the year.

Where to study the BPTC

The BSB has a list of validated BPTC course providers at www.barstandardsboard. org.uk/qualifying-as-a-barrister/bar-professional-training-course. Contact details for each of these course providers is also available from the BSB. There are currently only 11 institutions validated to provide the BPTC around the country, all of which offer a very high standard of tuition. There are more BPTC course providers in London than elsewhere, which is perhaps not surprising given that the majority of practising barristers are based in London. There is, however, nothing to stop you choosing to study the BPTC at any of the other providers, based in Bristol, Manchester, Nottingham, Leeds and elsewhere.

When you have completed the barristers' Vocational Stage of training, you are eligible to start your professional training, as a barrister's pupil. Note that being called to the Bar is not the same as qualification as a practising barrister.

A note on the proposed BSB aptitude test

You should be aware that the BSB has piloted an aptitude test for prospective BPTC students, to assess whether applicants to the BPTC have the skills needed to successfully complete the BPTC and go on to a career at the Bar. This has come as a response to the fact that there are many more BPTC students than there are pupillage places available (see Chapter 1 for more details on this). The idea of a 'entry' test is to ensure that places on the BPTC are given to those students with the aptitude for a career as a practising barrister, to prevent students with no realistic prospect of getting pupillage from wasting their time and money. This is a controversial scheme – take a look at the BSB website for consultation responses, views and discussions: www.barstandardsboard.org.uk/qualifying-as-a-barrister/bar-professional-training-course/aptitude-test.

The test is likely to be introduced in the autumn of 2012, for students wishing to start the BPTC in September 2013.

BPTC course content

As we have seen, barristers are primarily engaged in litigation and dispute-related work, which shapes the nature of the BPTC course contents. The BPTC is intended to prepare law graduates for pupillage and for going on to work as practising barristers. The course is intensive and challenging, being made up of many elements taught and tested throughout the course, and at least one formal assessment each month.

Compulsory modules

Civil litigation

The module focuses on civil litigation procedure, civil evidence and remedies. Civil litigation cases are governed by the Civil Procedure Rules (the CPRs or *White Book*), which also govern court procedures and how evidence is managed and presented in trials. While rules of procedure are a fairly dry subject to teach and learn in absence of their practical application, they are of crucial importance in any civil dispute, at almost any stage of the dispute's development. Civil litigation teaching is usually through weekly classes, with assessment by multiple choice-style tests.

Criminal litigation

Criminal litigation and procedure in the magistrates' court, Crown court and youth court are covered, from first arrest of the suspect, to trial, appeal and sentencing. Admissibility of evidence makes up a large part of the course, including hearsay evidence, and evidence obtained illegally. The main reference work for criminal law and procedure is *Blackstone's Criminal Practice*, which is referred to throughout the course, giving good exposure to one of the essential reference works used in criminal practice.

Opinion writing and drafting (two modules)

The barrister's spiritual home may be in court, but often more time is spent giving written advice on the merits of a claim (from either side's points of view) and how a case might best be conducted, usually on the instruction of a solicitor. Good drafting is therefore a crucial skill for a barrister. On the BPTC this is taught and assessed through drafting documents such as particulars of claim, defences to particulars of claim, responses to defences and preliminary injunctions. These are usually set in the context of contract- and tort-based problem scenarios.

Written exercises are set each week during the BPTC, with some providers allocating up to 20 sessions to opinion writing and drafting tuition throughout the course. Note that the opinion and drafting modules are now assessed through timed examinations at various points during the course, whereas on the BVC (the predecessor to the BPTC)these were take-home papers.

Conference skills

'Conference' – the formal name given to a meeting between a barrister and his instructing solicitor and/or client – is the main opportunity for a barrister to discuss a case face to face, in advance of a court or tribunal hearing. On the BPTC, conference skills are taught through scenarios, which can be based in either civil or criminal law, and in which any number of issues might arise. The barrister must be able to deal with all issues appropriately, and advise accordingly. The course is taught through weekly classes, with a final oral examination based on a combination of pre-prepared materials, and materials added during the assessment itself, with an actor playing the part of the solicitor/client.

Negotiation skills, and resolution of disputes out of court (two modules)

The cost, time and negative publicity often attached to court proceedings have together brought about an increase in alternative methods of dispute resolution (ADR). Barristers are increasingly being brought in to negotiate settlement with the opposing party. The negotiation module of the BPTC concentrates on good preparation and effective negotiation tactics, practised in the context of a civil claim where settlement can be achieved financially, through a sum of money being paid by one party to the other.

Mediation is another form of ADR and may be required in any number of legal contexts. A barrister may be required to represent a client in a mediation, or to advise on a form of dispute resolution that will be most effective to resolve a matter.

These modules are taught through weekly classes, and through practice negotiations with other BPTC students. As with the conference skills module, an actor plays the opposing barrister in the final assessment.

Advocacy

This is a key component of the BPTC, and covers applications to court, submissions in court, and handling witnesses. Applications to court may take the form of requesting a judge to grant a preliminary injunction, perhaps to prevent a neighbour from creating a nuisance. Witness handling usually takes the form of examination-in-chief and cross-examination of witnesses in court.

As with the negotiation skills module, advocacy is taught through a series of weekly interactive classes. Applications and witness handling are both assessed through oral examinations at the end of the term in which each module was taught, with actors playing the part of the judge, defendant or witness. Good advocacy skills are of such importance to barristers that some course providers allocate as much as 40 hours of tuition time to this part of the BPTC.

Professional ethics

This element of the BPTC looks at various professional ethical dilemmas that might be faced in practice, covering barristers' relationships with other members of the

Bar, lay clients (i.e. those who are not professionally qualified), professional clients and the courts. There is no discrete assessment in professional ethics. Instead, ethical issues are placed within other course module assessments (oral or written), with students being expected to identify ethical and conduct issues as they crop up, and to deal with them appropriately.

Professional and ethical conduct of the barristers' profession is set out in the Code of Conduct of the Bar of England and Wales (www.barstandardsboard.org.uk/regulatory-requirements/the-code of-conduct/).

Legal research and case preparation

The starting point for most legal problems, particularly those encountered early on in a barrister's career, is to research properly current case law and statutes relating to the problem. Legal research on the BPTC is structured to resemble the kinds of research tasks that might be encountered during pupillage. Problem questions are designed to require research using online resources (such as Westlaw and LexisNexis), and hard-copy resources (such as *Halsbury's Laws of England*). Research tasks are set on a weekly basis, culminating in a written exam, based around a pre-prepared problem scenario.

Optional modules

On completion of the compulsory modules, two further modules must be chosen to complete the BPTC. Most of these optional modules give insight into the legal and practical aspects of more specialised areas of practice, and serve as an introduction to the kinds of issues barristers may meet in the early stages of their career.

Some of the areas available as BPTC optional modules are:

- employment law

- company law

- family law

- international trade

- judicial review

- personal injury and clinical negligence

- property and chancery

- advanced criminal litigation.

These can be assessed in different ways, according to what is most appropriate for the subject matter. Some, such as company law and property, are assessed through written opinions on particular scenarios. Others might be assessed through practical oral exercises, such as an advocacy exercise for advanced criminal litigation, a conference with clients for family law, or a technical drafting exercise in the case of a judicial review scenario.

Advice on selecting optional modules on the BPTC, from a recent student

'Technically, it should not matter which optional modules you choose on the BPTC, as strictly you do not need to have studied these areas of law before doing the optional modules. My experience, however, was that if you were not familiar with the area of law covered in the optional module, then it was very difficult indeed to study. I would recommend only choosing modules with which you are at least reasonably comfortable, and with which you have some familiarity before you start.'

Modes of study

The BPTC can be taken as a one-year full-time course, with attendance required throughout the week, or a two-year part-time course with attendance at weekends. It is structured in two parts, with the compulsory modules taken first, followed by the two optional subjects.

Part-time or full-time?

Most course providers offer the BPTC as full-time or part-time courses. Full-time courses involve around 18 hours of formal teaching time per week, and as much private study time as is needed. Part-time BPTC courses usually consist of around 15 study weekends during the year, and require at least the equivalent of 30 hours of private study time per week.

Case study

Fredericka Argent is a non-practising barrister, and former BVC student. She has these views on how the BVC (now the BPTC) helped her in her later career

In terms of the work I do now, I have definitely found the procedural aspects of the law that I learned during the BVC very useful. For example, time spent learning the contents of the *White Book* has helped me apply the law in a much more practical way than I would have done had I only done an academic law degree without the extra year. My drafting skills are also much better following the BVC, which means I can be of more use to my employer when it comes to putting together the formal documentation that makes up a large part of our work.

Prior to the BVC, my writing experience was limited to essays, and I had never seen official court documents, forms and so on. I also learned important legal research skills on the BVC, including exactly where to look for specific information, and how to refine a search to make it as efficient as possible. These are apparently simple things, but they are crucial skills that the BVC has helped me develop. The main area that I have not had an opportunity to use since the BVC is advocacy, but all in all I feel that doing the BVC has definitely been beneficial to my career.

Summary

You now have a good idea of the kinds of subject areas and courses you will come across during the early stages of your legal career either as a solicitor or as a barrister. Each course provider gives detailed breakdowns of the various courses on their websites and in prospectus publications, so it's a good idea to look at a few different providers, to get an idea of how their teaching methods work, and to decide which one is likely to be best for you, before you sign up.

8

Extra-curricular opportunities while studying

While you are studying for your Graduate Diploma in Law (GDL), Legal Practice Course (LPC) or Bar Professional Training Course (BPTC), you have many opportunities to develop your CV, and to improve your career prospects by getting involved with extra-curricular groups and events. As the courses themselves are short (one year each for full-time students), it is essential that you research what is on offer right at the start of the first term (or earlier), and sign up to as many groups and activities that you think you will have time for, and which will directly benefit your CV. If a group does not exist in an area you are interested in, then start one. This demonstrates initiative and your commitment to building your experience.

Commercial awareness

If you are interested in commercial law, then all potential employers will expect you to demonstrate 'commercial awareness'. This is an elusive term, but it boils down to a few key points:

- understanding current commercial (i.e. non-legal) issues that affect both the wider economy and any sectors you are interested in

- showing that you have thought these issues through, and have an opinion on them

- understanding how a legal adviser's role relates to these commercial points, in the context of a client's business.

Working on your commercial awareness helps you to demonstrate that you can analyse issues from a commercial and legal perspective, and that you have the potential and interest to understand clients operating in different sectors, and the factors that influence their businesses. This will signal to interviewers and people reading your applications that you have the potential to become a lawyer who can offer good-quality, relevant legal services to clients. At the start of your legal career, just covering the course materials is not enough to convince an employer that you have what it takes. Future employers will be looking to see that you have taken the initiative, and will expect you to show evidence of broader skills that all good lawyers need.

Many students coming to law have not had a job before. If so, you may be wondering how to gain commercial awareness with only limited previous work experience. One answer is to get involved in commercial law groups and other activities, as you do your law courses. Attending seminars and lectures outside your courses is a good way of networking and keeping up to date on current developments – and it is even better if you can help organise these events. If you join an organising committee, you will benefit from the content of the seminars themselves, and, more importantly, you will be able to influence which speakers are invited, make contact with them directly, and impress them with your professionalism and organisational abilities. You can then add them to your network of relevant legal or commercial contacts, which will help when applying for training positions or other legal work. We will look at commercial awareness in the context of interviews in Chapter 11.

Another answer is to consider part-time work while studying. This would of course need to be balanced with your studies, and you need to ensure that you do not take on too much.

Advocacy experience

Pro bono work

If you are interested in advocacy and court work, then it will be expected that you have some experience in doing this – getting involved in a pro bono group is the ideal opportunity for you to represent and help people with all manner of real-life legal issues.

Pro bono groups exist at most of the major course providers, with the purpose of offering free legal advice to those who need it, on all kinds of different legal issues, including family law, housing, criminal and employment law. Student volunteers are supervised by qualified practitioners, and may be required to interview clients and to provide written or oral advice. Some pro bono units are affiliated with local councils. This creates a link with the local community, and offers an insight into the importance of advising the client on the legal issues that are relevant to them, while managing relationships with a number of interested parties.

Mooting

Most colleges and course providers offer the opportunity to get involved in mooting. This gives students the opportunity to develop their advocacy skills through arguing their case compellingly, on their feet. Mooting requires the ability to analyse a case, research related case law and legal principles, and present a legal argument clearly and coherently. It is an adversarial process, requiring quick reactions to the opponent's arguments, to convince the presiding judge to decide in your favour. Mooting competitions are organised around the country, allowing you to test your advocacy against new opponents, and perhaps to raise your profile by winning prizes or awards. Mooting events are also an excellent opportunity to meet barristers and judges, who often act as adjudicators and who may become useful professional contacts in the future.

Other activities

All course providers and colleges have a number of other groups through which you can build additional experience for your CV. If you have not yet decided on a course provider or college, then make sure you take potential extra-curricular programmes on offer into account when you are looking into which one to choose. These do not all have to be law-related, and can be used to demonstrate a range of skills that legal recruiters are looking for. For example, if you were on a social committee that organised an end-of-year ball, this will have required teamwork, organisation, time and budget management, negotiating with and managing people, and possibly even some commercial dispute resolution in a real-life context. However, do be aware that a lot of recruiters find this example very obvious and common, so be as creative as you can with your examples.

Acting, music and sport are other areas that involve interaction with others, project management, and a certain amount of work and discipline in order to achieve results. Make sure all this experience goes on your CV in a way that really sells the experience as something positive. And even if, in your opinion at least, something that you worked on was not the success you hoped it would be, there is always something positive to be said in terms of how you managed preparation and organisation, and what you learned from the experience.

Networking

A high proportion of jobs and training positions are offered to people who have made the effort to build a connection with an employer, be that a law firm, chambers or other organisation. This may seem on the surface to be evidence that perhaps the profession has not yet shaken off its elitist image, favouring people from familiar, connected backgrounds. If you do not have any contacts yet in law, then you may be asking yourself how you are going to be able to progress your career, if contacts are so important.

In fact, anyone can build up a network of useful contacts. Getting involved with college or university groups that interact with areas of the profession you are interested in is a very good way of making some initial contacts. In addition to joining groups, speak to your tutors, and make sure you use your careers service.

Tutors and careers advisers are on hand to give advice on who to approach and how, and are armed with up-to-date contact information. They also know former students who may be working in areas you are interested in, and who may be happy to meet informally over a coffee, to discuss what your options may be.

All law course providers are offering professional qualifications, and are aware that in today's competitive marketplace their performance will be judged on the ultimate employability of their students. It is therefore in the colleges' interests to provide the best possible services to help students improve their chances of successfully progressing to the next level of qualification, and on into work; they will do all they can to help.

Making contacts and keeping them up

It may be appropriate in some situations to approach a potential contact 'cold', if they have published their contact details online, and to request politely if they might spare a moment to talk, as you would value their insight and advice. A carefully drafted email may well be all it takes to set up a meeting, and to give you the chance to gain an expert's view on whichever areas you find interesting, or may be seeking some guidance in. This may in turn lead to a chance to do some work shadowing, a mini-pupillage or placement, or, perhaps, ultimately a job offer.

Ongoing contact with people you may have met in this way is quite an art, and there are no hard and fast rules that govern how you should keep in touch. When is a good time to get back in touch with a contact? The occasional email may be good, particularly if you have some good news to share, such as a good exam result. If your contact has recently had something published, or has been mentioned in the press, then this might create a good opportunity to re-establish contact. Use your initiative, be tactful, and you will find that there are a lot of people out there who are prepared to help you, and who will be impressed by your efforts. Who knows, one of these contacts may know of a vacancy or a role – either now, or years down the line – that you would not otherwise have known about, and which might be just what you are looking for.

Experience shows that, generally, people working in law at all levels are prepared to help others on their way up through the profession. They all understand the challenges, as they have been through the same process themselves. If you approach people politely and professionally, the chances are that they won't mind sparing some time to talk to you and offer some advice, even if only by way of a quick email. Do your research, and see who is already doing what you want to do. A wealth of information is available on law firm websites, while social networking services such as LinkedIn, Twitter and Facebook are excellent sources of additional information, and potential contacts.

Social networking or career suicide?

Social networking services are being used increasingly to vet potential applicants in all professions, so be careful with photos and comments you put up on Facebook and other social networks. The chances are that your future employer is looking at your pages with as keen an interest as your friends – so don't say or publish anything that might later come back to haunt you!

9

Managing your studies

Balancing work and life outside study

Workload and time management

It almost goes without saying that the best way to balance studying with other things in your life is to be highly organised, and to manage your time effectively. Everyone does this differently, and what works for some people will not work for others. The Academic and Vocational stage courses cover such a broad range of elements that inevitably some people will find some parts harder than others, even within the same class or study group. What matters is to make sure you keep on top of the courses as you go. The Graduate Diploma in Law (GDL), the Legal Practice Course (LPC) and the Bar Professional Training Course (BPTC) all cover a huge amount of ground in a short period of time, and the key to doing well in the assessments is to keep up with all the work as each course module progresses. Identify issues and difficulties as they arise, and deal with them as you go, rather than leaving them to the end; when it comes to revising for the exams and other assessments, you need to be sure you are relatively happy with everything covered before you start the revision. There will be plenty of questions and queries that you will need to go over before the exams, without having to use valuable revision time to tackle any missed modules, or areas you didn't cover properly the first time.

Below are some practical pointers, from successful GDL, LPC and BPTC students.

Treat studying like a job

If you are studying full-time, then treat all your courses as if they were a full-time job. If your classes are in the morning, stay in college and work in the afternoons to prepare for the following day. You may have other commitments, but if you do your best to put the hours in on an ongoing basis, this will help enormously in covering as much ground as possible at a sensible pace, without rushing to catch up.

Balance work and studying carefully

If you are studying part-time and working, then you do not have the luxury of being able to treat your studies like a full-time job – you probably already have one! There will be occasions when it will be hard to balance your career work with your academic work. Part-time courses are designed specifically with working people in mind, and your tutors will have seen students dealing with similar difficult situations to any you might face, and will know how to help. If you are having problems keeping up, then speak to your tutors as soon as you can. They can offer practical advice and guidance to help keep you on track, and can help you with any administrative issues, such as rescheduling classes or assessments. You should also keep your employer updated with your progress, and give them regular updates on how you are getting on. The most appropriate way of doing this will depend on the employer, but by making sure that they are aware of positive progress as well as potential issues, they will be better able to help you if any problems do crop up.

Make time for your social life

Whether studying full-time or part-time, you will have family and other social commitments which are not related to your legal work. No matter how hard you work, and how focused you are on doing the very best you can, it is essential to make time for life outside law. Family and friends are the best support network you have, and even if you feel fully engaged with your work, there is still a long way to go when you are still at law school. You'll be making a lot of friends and contacts, but be careful to pace yourself, and to make time for people who know you best. There is a lot to cover in the courses, and the temptation may be to spend every available moment studying, but you won't function well without contact from the outside world. Time spent with friends and family will help keep things in perspective, and keep your energy levels and morale up, even during more challenging times.

Spread out the workload

When studying, the temptation can sometimes be to put your head down and plough through as much material as you can in one sitting. It is well known that you can concentrate fully for only a couple of hours at a time, so make sure you take regular breaks as you work. If possible, go outside and stretch your legs for 10 minutes or so. Fresh air is a good cure for lapses in concentration, and it's important to give your eyes a rest from peering at books, or looking at a computer screen.

Get organised

When organising your time, set specific times aside for specific activities. If you have coursework to do as well as your training contract or pupillage applications, or contact emails to write or follow up, make sure you have earmarked time slots for each thing you need to do. It's best to slightly overestimate how long each thing will take you, to allow time for breaks, and for slippage if something takes longer than you think.

Use university holidays and consolidation weeks when there is no scheduled teaching to get on top of everything as the course progresses. This does not apply only to covering course content, but to your own admin as well. Organise your files, your revision notes, your tutorial and lecture notes, etc. while your timetable is free: it will save valuable time when revising.

Make the most of online resources

Some courses now offer online lectures and tutorials. Make use of the flexibility that these can offer – you can choose a time and place to suit you, which can be very useful in cutting down on travel time to college, or having to wait until a lecture or class is scheduled. This can help save travel costs, too.

Keep your notes, files and books

Make sure you keep all your notes and course materials for every course you do, after you have completed them. You will find that you need to refer back to these throughout the early stages of your career, particularly for the Academic and Vocational stages. You may find some of your LPC or BPTC notes give a good overview of something that you are about to work on during your training contract or pupillage, and may serve as a convenient reminder. All the course materials link together and are designed to reflect real-life legal work, so don't lose them (or be tempted to throw them away) as you go from one stage to the next.

Prepare for exams from the start of each course

On any of the law courses, it is not possible to leave the work to the last minute, as the various course elements relate to each other and join up as you go.

On the GDL, you have seven courses to consolidate for exams, in a very short period of time. GDL results are 70% exam-based, so your final grade will depend on your performance in the seven exams at the end of the course. Make sure you are prepared for these exams from the very start. Most course providers will offer mock exams at various stages of the courses, and while these are voluntary, they are the best way to assess your progress, to identify your weaker areas, and to get you used to doing legal exams under timed conditions. You will do better in some areas than others, but an early 'wake-up call' will give you the chance to focus on areas to work on while you still have time. Speak to your tutors about any particularly difficult areas as you go along, as they are there to help, and want you to succeed. There is more on exam strategy below.

The LPC and BPTC are both structured in two parts: the compulsory modules followed by optional modules. All the teaching and assessments for the first part are done in the first few months, after which you leave them behind. You then move on to the teaching and assessments for the second part. This gives very little time for consolidation, so you have to consolidate as you go. It is much harder to focus on the new course areas if you need to retake any exams or assessments at the same time.

Practise, practise, practise

The LPC and BPTC are very assessment heavy throughout the year, and there are exams and assessments at the end of both compulsory and elective/optional stages.

This can be quite a shock for those coming from undergraduate law degrees, where more time was available to consolidate each course module during the three years. With these courses, it is not possible just to put your head in the books and rely on being good on paper: we saw earlier that the interviewing and advocacy assessments are oral, while others are practical research tasks, using online or library resources, to teach and test a range of skills. Again, take advantage of the opportunities offered to practise these in good time, before the assessments themselves.

Dealing with law exams

Everyone working in any qualified legal position has sat a huge number of exams along the way. There are no exceptions to this, so it's important to do your homework on exam strategy. Law exams generally test your ability to identify and apply specific legal concepts to factual scenarios. You have to know the law, you have to be able to work through the questions to identify the issues from the facts presented, and you are then required to formulate an accurate, coherent answer. Some aspects of the law are very closely prescribed, to the extent that there can be a right or wrong answer. Other areas may have a little more capacity for your own interpretation, but generally you will be marked on fairly strict criteria, and there is no room for waffle.

Plan a proper revision schedule and stick to it

It is essential to work to a properly planned revision schedule. Allocating realistic time slots (mornings, afternoons, whole days) to the elements of a course will give you a road map with which you can navigate your progress through to exam day. If exams are scheduled in a batch, then some people find it useful to arrange revision in reverse order, revising for the latest exams first, then working back to revise for the earliest exams at the end of the revision period. That way, it is a relatively straightforward job to go back over the revision for each subsequent exam as they come along. You have already covered the material, and just need to go back over your notes before the exam.

Use summary cards

Condense your notes into summary cards containing the key information for each module or subject area, and test yourself on them as you go through the course.

Summaries are essential to revise from, and provide a quick overview of a course in a format that is easily memorised, and which should not be too daunting to look over. This helps boost your confidence when you look over the course material in the run-up to exams.

Know the format of each exam paper

Law exams differ greatly from subject to subject, so it is really important to know exactly what the format of each paper will be. How many sections are there? What is in each section (essays, problem questions)? What choice of questions do you have? Do you need to answer two of three questions? One of four? Are they essays or problem questions? You also need to know how many marks are available for each section, and for each question, so you can plan exactly how long you need to allocate in the exam for each. This is easy to plan, but very hard to stick to under time pressure: in the exam room, put your watch on your desk, so you can check the time as you go.

Finish every paper

You need to make absolutely sure that you finish every exam you sit. You have to attempt all the required questions in any paper in order to cover 100% of the available marks. You can't score marks in questions you haven't answered, and neither can you gain marks beyond the maximum available in those you have answered. The only way to guarantee the highest possible mark is to attempt every question, and that means planning your time and answering all the questions.

Use your support network

Law exams can be a daunting prospect, but most people get through them without too many problems. Some people find that the best way to cope with the exams is to get a healthy balance between working alone and following up with colleagues on specific areas that are unclear. One GDL class joked about having set up a 'revision hotline' before the exams: they would call each other at the end of each day's revision, to go over any points that were not clear. Almost every time, at least one person in the group would have understood a point that another had not, or had understood it in a slightly different way to the others. This made it easier to share difficult points with others who had not grasped them fully, in a clearer and more time-efficient way than going over course notes or textbooks alone. By working in this way, gaps and grey areas are quickly closed off, while keeping up vital morale and team spirit as exams approach. Your course provider will organise revision sessions for all assessments, which you should always attend, even if they are voluntary.

Dealing with open-book exams

Some law courses include open-book exams, particularly for certain elements of the LPC. Open-book exams are a relatively recent development and can seem strange and unfamiliar. The best way to approach an open-book exam is to consolidate your course materials well in advance, and to revise as if you could not take the materials into the exam. Taking reference materials into an exam may appear to make the exam easier; in fact, it sets a very easy trap to fall into, as you cannot rely solely on the materials you have, and you risk wasting time looking things up. Marks are not awarded for copying sections from the books, and you need to focus on analysing the questions, applying the relevant law, and giving a properly considered and structured answer.

Your revision notes are the best reference material to take with you into the exam, as they will be accurate, concise and easy to navigate. Mark these up with specific page numbers and tabs for quick reference if needed in the exam, but use them only as a prompt, not as an initial point of reference.

Working with materials provided in advance of exams or assessments

You may be provided with pre-assessment materials to review a few weeks before an exam. There will be certain restrictions on how you approach these, and you will probably not be permitted to discuss the materials in detail with tutors or colleagues. You will be able to do all the research you need in good time, to be able to answer the questions fully in the exam, so use the time you have as efficiently as possible. You may only be permitted to take a marked-up copy of the original pre-assessment document into the exam, so make notes on separate sheets first. Only add consolidated notes to the original after you know exactly what you need to have noted for the exam.

On the day of the exam

Last minute 'touching up' revision can make a big difference to your performance in an exam. Obviously, leaving anything other than overview revision to the last minute is a sure-fire way to failure, but going over your consolidated summaries the night before an exam, and for a couple of hours just before you take your seat on the day, can help boost your confidence. It can push the course content to the front of your mind, and ensure that any fiddly details, sequences or patterns of information can all be recalled as soon as they are needed. In the exam itself, there is nothing to stop you jotting down a few notes as soon as you are allowed to pick up your pen at the start – but don't get carried away!

Practical points

Law exams are often sat in conference centres or other large facilities to accommodate huge year groups, and these may be in locations away from your college that you do not know. Before all exams in unfamiliar locations, you must know where you are going well in advance. Use Streetmap or Google Earth to locate the venue, and to get an idea of what the area is like, so you don't get lost when you get there.

Work out your route, and how long the journey will take. Exams are important, and you don't want to risk any problems that might knock your concentration or leave you flustered. If you would usually take public transport or drive, then consider taking a taxi instead, booked to pick you up in good time. You can revise on the journey, and you will minimise the risk of getting lost or delayed. Finally, make sure you've eaten before the exam, and, if you can, take some chocolate or an energy bar with you, as well as a bottle of water.

Summary

These are just a few of the tried and tested methods that have been proven to make a positive difference when coping with the pressure of GDL, LPC and BPTC exams. There is plenty more material available to help you manage your exam strategy; look online or in your college library, and make sure you talk to one of your course tutors if you have any questions or concerns. *Student Essentials: Revision and Exam Strategies* by Mary Wickham (Trotman, 2011) is another good resource, with useful information in a handy format.

10

The professional stage: training positions explained

Introduction

When you have successfully completed the Academic and Vocational stages of training, you will be eligible to go on to complete the professional stage of training: by completing a training contract for solicitors, or a barrister's pupillage. These are the final stages of training before you qualify.

As a trainee solicitor or pupil barrister, the first few months are spent assisting your supervisors with their practical, day-to-day work. This introduces you to aspects of life as a working lawyer, and while the precise nature of the work will vary by department or supervisor, and according to the kinds of matters being worked on at any particular time, you can expect to be working on a range of different matters relating to a number of different areas of law. You will receive appropriate supervision, but you will also get a good deal of responsibility for the work allocated to you.

Thoughts from a trainee in a City firm

'Securing a training contract can be very, very hard work, and quite soul destroying when rejections keep coming in, but this is the same in any profession where there is a lot of competition for places. It's only when you're doing your training contract that you realise how great an opportunity it really is. Unlike other professions like accountancy, you don't have continuous assessments and exams as you work. With a training contract or pupillage, you learn through the practical work you do, a bit like an apprenticeship. As long as you work hard, and satisfy the requirements set by the SRA or BSB, then by the time you're doing your professional legal training, you will have no more exams to do in order to qualify, which is great.'

Trainee solicitors may be given responsibility for managing their own clients and matters after a month or two in each 'seat' (see page 158), or they may find themselves working on larger matters that prevent them from taking on their own files. Trainees are usually expected to have direct supervision from a partner up to qualification, and often for some time later. Pupil barristers generally spend six months working with a pupil supervisor before going on to manage their own workload, with less direct supervision. The process for barristers is similar, but usually takes one year, divided into two parts: six months under closer supervision from a suitably qualified barrister, and six months acting in a more independent capacity.

Before looking at how to get a training position, you need to know exactly what you are applying for. This is to make sure your applications are as good as they can be, and to show the employer that you have what they are looking for. There is quite a lot of information in this section, and you may think this might wait until you start your training. However, if you are to have a realistic chance of securing a place, you need to know what will be involved, so it is well worth familiarising yourself in some detail with what is usually covered in a training contract or pupillage. We will look at each one separately.

Solicitors' training contract

Objective

To complete your qualification as a solicitor, you will need to complete:

- a formal training contract with a supervising firm

- the Solicitors' Professional Skills Course (PSC; including optional Higher Rights of Audience qualification)

- a Criminal Records Bureau (CRB) check

- enrolment with the Solicitors Regulation Authority (SRA) as a solicitor.

Training contract eligibility

- Completion of the Academic Stage and solicitors' Vocational Stage of training (LPC).

- Enrolment with the SRA as a trainee solicitor.

How to apply for a training contract

- Applications are usually made direct to solicitors' firms. Check the firm's website, or make contact with firms to check how they prefer applications to be made.

- Many of the larger firms have online forms with fixed deadlines, after which applications are closed.

- Some firms prefer a CV and covering letter. There may be some flexibility as to timing of applications with firms that do not use an online system. Again, check with the firm to find out their requirements.

See Chapter 11 for more information on training contract applications.

ADDLESHAW GODDARD

DiFFeRENT

See your career in a different light

Help us grow as a team. We'll help you grow as an individual.

As a fast expanding and innovative law firm, a career with Addleshaw Goddard means more variety, earlier responsibility and greater future opportunities to develop with the firm. Training with us will mean working with top FTSE companies and other leading organisations.

With offices in London, Leeds and Manchester, we can offer quality training wherever you want to be based. If you are interested in a training contract with us or a Summer/Easter placement visit:

www.addleshawgoddard.com/graduates

www.addleshawgoddard.com

Profile: Addleshaw Goddard

ADDLESHAW GODDARD

As a major force on the legal landscape, Addleshaw Goddard offers extensive and exciting opportunities to all its trainees across the entire spectrum of commercial law, from employment and banking to real estate, corporate finance, intellectual property, PFI and litigation. As a trainee with this firm, you'll be a key member of the team from day one. Wherever you are based, you'll work closely with blue chip clients within a supportive yet challenging environment, and be part of a structured training programme designed to ensure your success – now and in the future.

Main areas of work

The firm has five main business divisions: finance and projects, litigation, commercial services, corporate and real estate. Within these divisions, as well as the main practice areas it also has specialist areas such as intellectual property, employment and private client services such as trusts and tax.

Trainee profile

Graduates who are capable of achieving a 2.i and can demonstrate commercial awareness, teamwork, motivation and drive. Applications from law and non-law graduates are welcomed, as are applications from students who may be considering a change of direction. We also have a Legal Access scheme for applicants on GDL or LPC with less conventional academic backgrounds. Further details can be found on our website.

Training environment

During each six-month seat, there will be regular two-way performance reviews with the supervising partner or solicitor. Trainees may have the opportunity to spend a seat in one of the firm's other offices and there are a number of secondments to clients available. Being seated with a qualified solicitor or partner and working as part of a team enable trainees to develop the professional skills necessary to deal with the demanding and challenging work the firm carries out for its clients. Practical training is complemented by high-quality training courses provided by both the in-house team and external training providers. A trainee buddy programme is in place with the trainee predecessor for the first seat. All trainees have a mentor for the duration of their training contract and beyond.

Sponsorship and benefits

GDL and LPC fees are paid, plus a maintenance grant of £7,000 (London) or £4,500 (elsewhere in the UK). Benefits include corporate gym membership, season ticket loan, subsidised restaurant, pension and private healthcare.

Vacation placements

Places for 2013: 70
Duration: 1 or 2 weeks
Location: all offices
Apply by: 31 January 2013
Interviews for our vacation schemes start in early January

Locations

Milton Gate, 60 Chiswell Street, London EC1Y 4AG

Sovereign House, Sovereign Street, Leeds LS1 1HQ

100 Barbirolli Square, Manchester M2 3AB

In 2012 we opened up an office in Singapore, with an office in Dubai set to open later this year.

Website: www.addleshawgoddard.com/graduates

Key info

Partners: 160

Associates: 500+

Trainees: 70

Contact: grad@addleshawgoddard.com

Closing date for 2015: 31 July 2013

Interviews for our training contracts start in early June

Training contracts: 30 per year

Applications: 2,000 per year

Percentage interviewed: 8%

Required degree grade: 2.i

Case study

A day in the life of an Addleshaw Goddard trainee

Aneesa Hussain is a third seat trainee in the acquisition finance team of the banking division.

The account below is by no means a typical day, as any Addleshaw Goddard trainee will tell you: no two days are the same. I am currently working on a large, multi-jurisdictional deal where our lender client is lending funds to a borrower to fund its acquisition of a target group of companies. Today's tasks mostly focus on this one deal.

9a.m.: I skim news stories online, respond to emails and add to the 'to do' list I created yesterday. All of this is complemented by a cup of tea!

9.30a.m.: I arrange a progress call with the associate on the borrower's legal team to discuss the conditions to lending imposed by the lender, known as Conditions Precedent (CPs) and which of these CPs is outstanding. After the call I update the CP list and inform my supervisor about progress before circulating it to all parties.

10.30a.m.: The borrower's overseas counsel have produced numerous due diligence reports relating to the target companies. Yesterday I drafted and circulated some language to allow our client to rely upon these reports. The borrower's overseas counsel have responded with letters of reliance incorporating all, some, or none of my drafting. I review and amend the letters to strengthen our client's position and I leave the marked-up letters with an associate to review.

12.30p.m.: A training session is being delivered by the Leeds commercial team via video conference on the topic of intellectual property rights in banking deals. After the training I head to the AG restaurant for a quick lunch with a couple of trainees.

2p.m.: Back at my desk, I reply to emails that require immediate responses and flag those that I can deal with later.

2.30p.m.: Yesterday I circulated a new version of the loan agreement (from the acquisition deal) to our overseas counsel and by now they have all responded with comments, which I review. I call German counsel for clarification of several points, then talk my supervisor through proposed amendments. Afterwards, I give my PA the amendments to incorporate.

3.30p.m.: I have several post-completion tasks for a deal that completed recently. To minimise time client costs, I instructed our transaction services team in Manchester to produce an e-bible, which I now review and amend. I also collate the original executed documents and send them to the print room to be bound.

4.30p.m.: My PA hands me the loan agreement incorporating the amendments, which I proofread then circulate to the borrower's solicitors.

5p.m.: I speak to the associate who reviewed my marked-up letters of reliance and she is happy for me to send these.

5.15p.m.: I am arranging a CSR (corporate social responsibility) event and call the external facilitator to discuss any outstanding points. I follow up with an email and send emails to our catering, audio-visual and facilities teams to outline their tasks.

5.45p.m.: I respond to emails that relate to another matter and work through flagged emails in my inbox.

6.30p.m.: I had sent an email to overseas counsel some days ago requesting an update of how much of their fee estimate they have used to date. With responses from everyone, I create a status table for the client, which I show to my supervisor before sending.

7.15p.m.: As there are no other urgent tasks, I ensure my time recording is up to date, create my 'to do' list for tomorrow and then leave.

Advice from a partner in a City firm: Daniel Turnbull of Stewarts Law LLP

'Nowadays, training contracts seem to be like gold dust. It is quite rare to secure one during your law degree, on the GDL or even on the LPC. The reality is that it's not unusual to see people start a training contract in their late twenties or even thirties. My advice is to get as much legal experience as you can, particularly through paralegalling. Often this opens doors in a firm; the firm sees how you work and gets to know you well. Many firms are recruiting from within like this.

'You should try to get as many strings to your bow as possible, including in non-legal areas such as business development. This is important for any career, not just law, as you have to learn how to be confident with people, and build a network of contacts. An excellent way to get this experience is through working with charities, or volunteering. Working with other organisations like these gives you a range of experience, and can really give you the edge over another applicant. This looks good on your CV, and will greatly improve your chances of getting a training contract.'

When to apply for a training contract

- Training contracts usually start in September, while some of the larger firms take an additional intake the following March, allowing candidates time between the end of the LPC and start of the training contract. March starters will therefore qualify in March two years later, six months after the September intake.

- For mid-sized and top-tier law firms, applications are required to be submitted at the end of July, two years before the training contract is due to start. For example, applications for a training contract due in 2015 would need to be submitted in July 2013. For undergraduates, this means submitting applications between the second and third years of their degree. For non-law graduates, applications will need to be submitted a few months **before** the GDL starts, in order to allow you to progress directly from the GDL to the LPC, and on to your training contract.

- Some firms have separate application processes for law graduates and for non-law graduates. Non-law graduates may be required to apply earlier than law graduates.

- Each firm has its own individual application process, so you should check carefully what is required and when, for each firm you intend to apply to.

- High-street and smaller firms may recruit much nearer to the start date of the training contract, and often recruit during the LPC year.

Deadlines and lead times

Note that training contract application procedures and deadlines vary from firm to firm, so you must ensure you know the deadlines and requirements well in advance for every application you make. Missing a deadline may mean you end up having to wait another year before you can apply again. As noted above, it is common for training contract applications and offers to be made two years before the training contract starts: this goes back to the days when most people came to law straight from undergraduate law degrees. The majority of training contract offers were made in the second year, to allow a year for finals, and a year for the LPC.

Today, more people come to training contracts from other routes, and for many, the two-year lead time can be a significant obstacle in the way of career progress. The lead time means that non-law graduates are required to apply for a training contract before they have studied any law. You need to bear this in mind when you are planning your career, as you may find yourself with at least a year's gap to fill, particularly for GDL students who are unable to secure a training contract during the GDL year. This can be turned to your advantage, however. Use the time to gain legal work experience, perhaps working as a paralegal (see page 69). This experience may even count towards your training (see below). You need to be aware that you might need to be flexible in your planning, as it is not always possible to progress from the LPC directly to a training contract. The same goes for BPTC students looking for pupillage.

Relevant work experience

Relevant legal work experience may count towards your training contract and may allow you to reduce the duration of your training contract from the usual two years. The SRA has further information on this, and you should discuss this with the firm with whom you are intending to train.

Preparing for qualification

In order to qualify as a solicitor, trainees are required to apply for full SRA membership. This includes arranging admission to the roll of solicitors, and your first practising certificate, upon payment of a fee. More details are available on the SRA website at www.sra.org.uk.

Trainees are also required to complete a Criminal Records Bureau (CRB) check. This is to check if any prospective solicitors have a criminal record, and, if so, what the status of any penalties is. If you have a criminal record, this is likely to affect your eligibility to qualify. Detailed guidance is available from the CRB when you come to fill in the form. This is usually done about three months before the end of the training contract. More information on CRB checks is available at www.homeoffice. gov.uk/agencies-public-bodies/crb.

How training contracts work, and what is involved

Training contracts are usually two years long (unless qualifying through the Chartered Institute of Legal Executives (CILEx) route, see below), with time spent in different departments of the firm. The objective is to achieve standards set by the SRA, through gaining practical experience in the following areas:

- advocacy and oral presentation

- case and transaction management

- client care and practice support

- communication skills

- dispute resolution

- drafting

- interviewing and advising

- legal research

- negotiation.

You will gain some experience in all these areas during your training, to varying levels, according to the work coming through the department in which you are sitting, or on which your supervisor is working.

Trainees are usually required to spend time in at least three different departments of the firm. Trainees working in firms with fewer departments may find themselves as a shared resource across the firm. Those working in larger firms will usually have their time divided into units of four or six months, known as 'seats', in specific departments. The six-month seat system gives more detailed exposure to the work of each department, and an opportunity to become well acquainted with the matters you are working on. Seats of four months offer the opportunity to experience a broader range of work in more departments, and then to go back to a department you were particularly interested in.

Training record

The SRA requires all trainees to complete a record of the work they have done during their training contract to demonstrate that their work meets the SRA standards. The training record must include details of the work done, the particular skills covered (by reference to the SRA practice areas listed on page 158), observations on their own performance, and any professional conduct issues that might have come up. Further training or tuition received should also be noted, such as attendance at seminars or briefings, articles written or published, and so on.

The SRA is entitled to inspect law firms, to monitor their performance in how they train their trainee solicitors. You may be called upon at any time to produce your training record, so make sure you keep it updated as you go, to prevent you having to catch up later!

Secondments

Some firms send trainees on secondment to clients, which can be an excellent way of gaining hands-on working experience outside the firm's working environment. Secondments are also a great way of putting yourself on the map as an ambassador for your firm and a point of contact between the firm and the client. They look good on your CV, too.

Professional Skills Course

In addition to the day-to-day work covered during your training contract, all trainees must complete a compulsory Professional Skills Course (PSC) before they can be admitted as solicitors. The PSC is a practical course administered by the SRA, which covers many of the issues that are likely to come up in all areas of solicitors' practice. There are several modules to the PSC, the majority of which are often done in the first week of the training contract, before the first seat starts. The other modules are taken as your training contract progresses. As with the LPC, the PSC is made up of core modules and electives, with the core modules usually being completed first. However, unlike the LPC, the PSC is covered mainly by attendance at seminars, with only one short written assessment (see below).

Core PSC modules

Advocacy and communication skills

This module covers case preparation, analysis and presentation. Criminal and/or civil court cases are used as case studies, with classroom-based mock trials used to demonstrate and discuss advocacy techniques at the various stages of a hearing (opening and closing speeches, examination-in-chief, cross-examination).

Client care and professional standards

The objective of this module is to further improve understanding of professional conduct, beyond what was covered on the LPC. This includes analysis of the Solicitors' Code of Conduct, ethical issues and risk management, and dealing with situations that are likely to crop up in practice, such as handing duties to third parties and the court, undertakings and implications of giving them, and project management.

Financial and business skills

This course deals with the regulatory aspects of a solicitor's dealings with financial matters, and the rules governing when and how solicitors may give financial advice, by reference to the SRA Code of Conduct and regulatory regimes governing the provision of financial services, in particular the provisions of the Financial Services and Markets Act 2000 (FSMA). The PSC builds on the LPC in this area, and its importance is reflected in the fact that it is the only PSC module involving a written assessment. This is a multiple-choice exam of 1.5 hours, which tests the key areas covered in the course.

Elective PSC modules

You need to cover 24 further hours of PSC training through subjects appropriate to your areas of work, in order to complete the PSC. A minimum of 12 hours must be spent in face-to-face tuition, while the rest may be conducted by distance learning. PSC electives are usually taught classes or seminars, which are fitted around your other work as a trainee. Elective courses are available in all the main areas of a solicitor's work.

- Contentious electives include criminal, family and employment law, personal injury and dispute resolution.

- Non-contentious electives include corporate law, commercial property, commercial and intellectual property law, and private client law.

- Practice skills electives appropriate to all areas of practice include commercial law firm management, written and communication skills, negotiation and presentation skills.

For solicitor advocates, Higher Rights of Audience training counts towards the PSC requirements. This course can be done as either a trainee or a qualified solicitor, and is a qualification in its own right, aside from the other electives. More information on the qualification process for solicitor advocates is available from the Society of Solicitor Advocates (see www.solicitoradvocates.org).

Contentious and non-contentious work

The SRA requires trainees to gain a balance of contentious and non-contentious experience as they cover the practical areas above (see page 63 for more information). If your firm (or employer, if you are training in-house) cannot offer you experience in a particular area, they can arrange for you to go on secondment to a firm that can offer this experience. If, for example, you are training in-house in a company, then it is possible that you will not gain experience in litigation or dispute resolution. In this case, a secondment to a law firm's litigation department for a few months will give you the experience the SRA requires.

ALLEN & OVERY

Setting precedents, not following them.

At Allen & Overy you will have to be able to think beyond what has been done before. You'll be supporting ambitious businesses that are themselves breaking new ground and your ideas can make the difference. So, from your first day as a trainee – and even as a student on a vacation scheme – what you do and say will matter, both to your team and to your clients.

Visit **www.allenovery.com/careeruk** to see more.

Join Allen & Overy to do more.

www.facebook.com/AllenOveryGrads

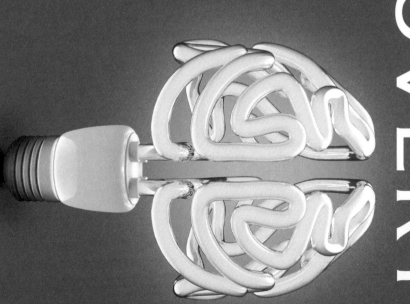

Profile: Allen & Overy

ALLEN & OVERY

About Allen & Overy

Allen & Overy LLP is an international legal practice working in 42 major centres worldwide. Our clients include many of the world's top businesses, financial institutions and governments.

Start at the top

Starting your career with Allen & Overy means starting at the very top of international commercial law. We are renowned for the high quality of our banking, corporate and international capital markets advice, but also have major strengths in areas such as litigation and dispute resolution, employment and benefits, tax and real estate.

Training

We offer a truly flexible training contract and the most interesting work in a unique culture of support and mutual respect. The seat structure ensures that you get to see as many parts of the practice as possible and that your learning is hands-on, guided closely by an associate or partner. Most seats are for six months, with some three-month seats available. Given the strength of our international finance practice, we require our trainees to spend a minimum of 12 months in our core areas of banking, corporate and international capital markets. The firm offers its trainees the option of completing a litigation course. The course is run by Nottingham Law School and consists of five days' tuition and monthly visits to a legal advice centre for a year to gain practical contentious experience. In addition to the Professional Skills Course there are numerous training courses available covering a broad range of legal and personal skills.

Trainees have told us that one of the things they value most about being at Allen & Overy is the excellent training they receive.

Who we are looking for

We expect to see a strong, consistent academic performance with at least a 2.i (or equivalent) predicted or achieved. At Allen & Overy you will be working in a team where you will use your initiative and manage your own time and workload, so we also look for evidence of teamwork, leadership, motivation and problem-solving.

Working environment

Life at Allen & Overy is about more than just the work we do – our team environment encourages professional and social relationships. The Trainees' Social Committee is responsible for planning a variety of events, from drinks and theatre trips, to the annual trainee summer ball. There are also sports teams, a fully equipped fitness centre, music rooms and multi-faith prayer rooms.

Application dates for training contracts

To apply for our March and September 2015 intakes, you will need to visit www.allenovery.com/careeruk

Final year non-law undergraduates and graduates can apply from 1 November 2012 to 15 January 2013. Penultimate year law undergraduates and graduates can apply from 1 June 2013 to 31 July 2013.

'Allen & Overy LLP' refers to Allen & Overy LLP and/or its affiliated undertakings.

Case study

Adam Baldwin, third seat trainee (studied law at Southampton University)

I started my training contract with Allen & Overy in March 2011. However, my experiences with the firm date back to 2008. Whether it was through the summer vacation scheme, the sponsorship of the university rugby team or the friendships made on the bespoke LPC course, Allen & Overy featured as a significant part of my higher education and social life even before my first day at work, which truly reflects the ethos of the firm. I am now over a year into my working life at Allen & Overy and my experiences of the firm remain consistently positive.

I began work in the securitisation department, where the majority of my work revolved around the securitisation of Norwegian consumer loans. My role varied from reviewing comments from the other legal teams on the deal, to running conference calls and producing the first drafts of various security documents. It proved to be a great start to my training contract, providing exposure to some very high-level and technical aspects of law, but also allowing me to work on a deal from start to finish. I am currently on a client secondment. This has proven a fantastic hands-on experience, allowing me to put the skills developed over the last year to good use. The possibilities of a secondment at Allen & Overy, client or otherwise, was a major attraction to me pursuing a career with the firm.

The quality of training at Allen & Overy makes it stand out from many other firms. From day one there is a strong sense of support and development, be it in a legal, management, IT or 'soft skills' sphere. Trainees are regarded as an important future element of the firm and are treated in this regard accordingly. I am part of the Trainee Solicitor Liaison Committee, set up by the firm to provide a vehicle to convey ideas and issues from the trainee body up to the senior fee earners, reflecting the regard paid to trainees.

Allen & Overy is a place for 'development'. There is constant attention given to developing one's legal knowledge, with the regular occurrence of departmental seminars, briefings and updates. However, development goes beyond 'the books'. Allen & Overy realises that the business of our clients is as equally reliant on the people involved as it is on the information that those individuals apply to it. Therefore, trainees are given ample opportunity to meet with clients in both a business and social setting. I am part of the firm's rugby team; we often play against clients, providing a great opportunity to develop relationships beyond deals.

Within the firm, the well-being of trainees is highly valued. The office at Bishops Square caters for one and all. Starting your day with a workout in the firm's well-equipped gym, grabbing lunch at the in-house Italian trattoria and finishing the evening with a pint on the expansive terrace provide the perfect accompaniment to the best training contract on offer in the City.

Barristers' pupillage

As we mentioned earlier, barristers' pupillages last one year, and are divided into two six-month stages, known as 'sixes'. The first 'six' is referred to as the 'non-practising' six, since the pupil is not yet eligible to take on their own matters. Instead, they assist their pupil supervisor in case preparation, at hearings, conducting legal research, and observing the supervisor. In the second six, the pupil is eligible to take on his or her own matters, managing their own cases and clients. At this stage pupils start to develop their professional profile and reputation as practising barristers. When applying for pupillage, you need to bear this structure in mind, and demonstrate your capability to assist a pupil supervisor adequately for the first few months, before moving on very quickly to take on a good deal of work and responsibility yourself, in a relatively short period of time.

Objective

To complete your qualification as a barrister, you will need to complete:

- barristers' pupillage (one year spent training under a qualified barrister)

- compulsory training courses in advocacy, practice management and accounting.

Eligibility for obtaining pupillage

- Completion of the Academic Stage of training.

- Completion of the barristers' Vocational Stage of training (passing the BPTC or BVC) within the last five years.

- You will need to have been called to the Bar before you start pupillage.

How to apply for pupillage

The Pupillage Portal (www.pupillages.com – formerly the OLPAS system) allows candidates to submit applications to up to 12 barristers' chambers. The website also contains a list of all pupillages available, including those offered by chambers that are not part of the Pupillage Portal network.

See Chapter 1 for more information on how pupillage works.

When to apply for pupillage

- The Pupillage Portal operates to a very strict timetable, which is available at www.pupillages.com/help/PreLogon/olpas/timetable.asp.

- Pupillages usually start in September or October.

- The Pupillage Portal allows first applications for pupillages to be submitted *only* between the end of March and the end of April of each year, at which point the system closes to applicants.

- Applications are considered between May and September, with offers being made from early August to early September.

- The system closes altogether each year at the end of October, to reopen again for candidates the following March.

- Chambers that are not part of the Pupillage Portal network may be approached direct – check with each one for application requirements and deadlines.

- You must register your pupillage with your Inn and with the Bar Standards Board (BSB) before you start, in order for all of your pupillage time to count towards qualification.

Preparing for qualification

You will need to obtain formal Certification of Pupillage on completion of the first six months of pupillage (the non-practising element of professional training), and a second Certification of Pupillage after the second, practising, six months.

When you have completed all the necessary stages of pupillage, you will be issued with a Full Qualification Certificate. Note that this is not the same as a practising certificate, which must be obtained separately from the Bar Council.

There are four core areas in which the BSB sets requirements for experience and competence in all pupils:

- conduct and etiquette

- advocacy

- conferences and negotiations

- drafting, paperwork and legal research.

The BSB issues checklists for use by pupils and supervisors, which set out details of these core areas, and the skills that need to be covered during both first and second sixes. These can be adapted by individual chambers to reflect the precise nature of the work carried out, and chambers or supervisors will ensure that pupils gain the required experience as their pupillage progresses. For full details of the BSB requirements, consult the current version of the BSB's *Pupillage Handbook*, available at www.barstandardsboard.org.uk.

In addition to the core skills and checklists above, the Bar Council requires all barristers to have completed three formal training courses before a practising certificate will be issued:

- advocacy training

- practice management training

- forensic accounting.

These courses are organised by a pupil's Inn, rather than by chambers, and course elements vary from Inn to Inn. You can expect the courses to go well beyond the minimum requirements, often being covered in weekend residential courses. These courses are outlined below.

Advocacy training

A minimum of 12 hours of advocacy training is required during pupillage, and must be completed within the first six months. Advocacy training is mainly conducted through exercises in legal argument and speeches, and making or opposing applications to court, such as injunctions. Witness handling, case analysis, examination of witnesses and cross-examination are also covered. Advocacy is often tested through practical exercises in court, with a judge presiding over the exercise as if it were a true hearing.

Practice management training

This is made up of several elements, and is usually covered in the second six months of pupillage. Subjects included in the practice management course include:

- managing the transition from Bar student to independent practitioner

- professional ethics

- managing tenancy as a practising barrister

- court etiquette

- accounts and book-keeping

- working with Legal Aid.

You can also expect to receive training in specialist areas of the Bar, in which you may either wish to practise or are already practising. These include the areas of barristers' practice that we looked at in Chapter 4, as well as additional areas such as local government and planning law, technology and construction law, commercial and admiralty law, immigration law and revenue law.

Forensic accounting

The forensic accounting course is an introduction to financial accounting information as it applies to a barrister's work. The course covers the main principles of accounting and financial documents that are likely to be encountered in the context of litigation, and to enhance awareness of accounting systems in order to improve individual barristers' own practice.

11

Applying for a training position: how to approach employers

You now have an idea of what to expect during your training contract or pupillage. Armed with this knowledge, and after doing more of your own research into areas specific to your interests, you are ready to make a start on applying to firms or chambers, to obtain a training position. This is not an easy process, but with enough information, and good preparation, you will maximise your chances of success.

Where to start

As a starting point, for each application you make, whether you are a prospective solicitor or barrister, you need to demonstrate that:

- you have done your foundation research (see next page)

- you know where you want to go in your career

- you understand the employer's areas of work, areas of law covered, and its client base

- you understand the role you're applying for

- you understand what requirements and standards you need to meet

- you are confident that you can do a good job in that role

- you can give examples to back up what you say.

Here are some tips to help cover each of these areas, to help build your strategy to secure a place.

Foundation research and knowing where you want to go

Before you make any applications, think carefully about who the right employers really are for you. You must be sure that by the time you start to make applications, you have a fairly clear idea of the areas of law you want to work in, and therefore who your target firms or chambers are. Don't worry if you are not sure exactly where you ultimately wish to specialise, or if you are unsure which department you might want to qualify into. You need to keep an open mind as your training progresses, as the more experience you gain, the better informed you will be to make this decision on qualification. All that matters at the application stage is that you know the general direction that you want your career to head in – are you looking to do commercial law, or more family- or high-street-oriented work? Criminal or civil?

With tough competition for places, the temptation is to think that it doesn't really matter where you end up, as long as you are offered something. You must, however, go for what is right for you. Ultimately, it's your training, and you need to be sure that at the end of it you have gained experience and knowledge in areas that will be useful for the rest of your career. If you are confident that the role you are applying for will cover this, then you have a much better chance of convincing the employer of your suitability for that role.

Select a target group of employers to apply to, and focus on this group first. For solicitors this can be hard to do, for practical reasons. There are a lot of firms to choose from, and if there is a two-year lead time between applying for a training contract and starting it, this can make matters more complicated. However, with enough research and some work experience, you should have a good idea of which firms do the work you are interested in, and which ones are likely to be a good fit for you. Make a priority list, and apply to these first. You can go on to make further applications later, as necessary.

Understanding the employer's work

Law firms' and chambers' websites are invaluable sources of information on the kinds of work they do. These sites are designed to give a positive and clear picture of areas that they specialise in, with information on recent successes and significant developments, as well as more general information. You should study in detail the websites of all employers you are particularly interested in. They will be regularly updated, and it is important for every applicant to know what the latest developments are within that organisation. Have they been working on any major cases or commercial deals? Has one of their lawyers published something that relates to an area you are interested in?

It is often helpful to check the contacts sections, where lawyers mention their individual areas of expertise, and usually list a few recent matters they have worked on. When it comes to preparing for interviews, it can be very useful to put a face to the names of people you may meet, or who may interview you.

Go to law fairs, open days and other careers events. These give an excellent opportunity to speak with representatives of law firms or chambers, and to go over things face to face, rather than online. Trainees and pupils often attend law fairs on behalf of their employer, as well as HR staff or more senior lawyers. They are happy to talk about what they do, and this is an ideal opportunity for you to get first-hand information on what to expect from any role you apply for.

It's important to make a good impression with all potential employers you meet, and particularly those you are keen on applying to. You can do this by showing you already have some understanding of what they do, and how the organisation is structured. This may be from articles on careers websites or in publications, or just from a careful review of their own website. Being informed makes you stand out from the crowd. Use this as a basis from which to ask more detailed questions about areas of work, or the department of the particular person you are speaking to, and for any general advice or thoughts they may have for someone in your position.

You may find that it is possible to arrange a work placement or vacation scheme directly through contacts made at events like these. If not, you can at least find out in some detail what the application procedure is, and what they tend to look for in applicants for vacation placements and training positions.

Understanding the role

You can gain a good level of understanding of what to expect in any role you apply for from the employer's websites or from other publications, as mentioned above. However, you also need to have a good understanding of some of the more technical aspects of what is required at each stage of training, in order to make your applications as good as they possibly can be, and to ensure you are equipped with the knowledge you need for interviews. You will not be expected to know everything there is to know about law, but you should understand what your training will involve, and what the various stages and requirements are of a training contract or pupillage. Use the information earlier in this chapter as a starting point to research how the various training positions work at the places you are applying to. You will impress the recruiter if you show awareness of what is involved, and you can use this as a basis to demonstrate how and why you are suitable.

To gain an understanding of what the role is like, try to speak to current trainees or pupils. Very often they will attend law fairs, as mentioned above, and they will certainly attend open days and other events hosted by the employer. They are happy to discuss their experiences, and are well versed in successfully navigating the application process as a whole. They will have personal experience of their employer's application and interview procedures, and are ideally placed to give you some really useful insight into what the employer is looking for, and what worked for them. You should always bear in mind that a good impression made when speaking with any representative from any organisation may well be fed back and serve as a mark in your favour.

You should also make sure you are in regular contact with your college careers service, updating them with progress you are making with applications, and, in particular, letting them know which employers you have had contact with. Your careers advisers may know the firms or chambers you are applying to, and might be able to draw on the experience of past applicants to help give you further information and advice on what to expect from the application process. Some careers services ask students to feed back on their experiences at interviews and assessments (whether they have gone well or not so well!). These are kept on file, and can be an invaluable source of insider information on what the structure of the interview or assessment was, what kinds of questions were asked, who the interviewers were, and other details based on their experiences. This information can be a great advantage when approaching an employer, or preparing for an interview.

Understanding requirements and standards for entry

You need to satisfy the requirements of the role you are applying for. If you have a blip on your CV, or if you feel that further clarification is needed to explain your qualifications, you need to have a strategy in place to overcome this – see Chapter 6.

Being confident you can do a good job in the role

This is down to you as an individual. Once you have done all your foundation research, spoken with trainees or pupils, and you know where you are heading, it is likely that you have a good idea of what is involved in any particular training role, and that you are capable of doing it, and doing it well. Using clear, positive language is a good first step in demonstrating confidence in applications and getting your suitability for the role across to the person reading your application. Backing up your statements with relevant examples adds further weight to showing yourself off as a capable individual, and a credible candidate (see below). Using a similar strategy in interviews will also show you in your best light.

Using examples to support what you are saying

We will look at some of the common legal application and interview questions in more detail later. Legal applications and interviews are designed to be challenging, to find out about your achievements, and, perhaps more tellingly, also to understand how you are as a person, testing your powers of reasoning and argument, how you react under pressure, and so on. The employer is looking for these skills, and the application form or interview is your chance to demonstrate them.

However, it is not enough simply to say you are good at something, or that you enjoy a particular area of law and want to pursue it as a career. You must be able to back up what you say by drawing on relevant examples, preferably from your own experiences with the employer. If this is not possible, then you should set your answers in real-life, preferably law-related, contexts. Think about your legal experience so far: the best answers will draw from practical experience, and will link areas together, for example: 'I did a vacation scheme with your firm last summer, working in department B on matter C. I was responsible for tasks D and E, which involved using resources F and G, and skills H and I. I gained a good understanding of how areas of law J and K related to each other in the context of the matter, and what the commercial implications were for the client.' If you can back this up further with positive feedback from a supervisor, it will add weight to what you say.

Competition for places is tough, and you may need to think laterally as you progress with your applications. There will always be mainstream routes to qualification, via large law firms or the well-known barrister sets, but a wealth of alternative routes to qualification exists too. For example, some non-legal employers offer training schemes to staff working in-house. If a particular sector appeals to you more than the idea of working in legal practice, then you may be better off gaining some hands-on experience at graduate or paralegal level, before going on to train and qualify in-house. We will look at some alternative career plans in Chapter 12.

Making written applications

Practical points on applications generally

We will look at the kinds of questions that may be asked in application forms and interviews later in the chapter. Meanwhile, wherever you are applying, and whatever method of application you need to use, a few foundation rules apply.

Do your research (again!)

Revisit your research on the organisation you are applying to. Understand their core areas and competencies, how big they are, who their main clients are, and so on. Try to relate your experiences to the type of work they do. This goes back to commercial awareness – you need to show that you understand the organisation, the sectors it operates in and its clients, to be able to demonstrate that you are a good fit. They will know if you've done your research or not.

What are you saying?

You need to think very carefully about the information you submit in each and every application. Everything you say has to be relevant to the position you are applying for. You should expect to be asked rigorous or difficult questions about what you have said, so you must make sure you are able to back up everything you submit in every application. Make sure the examples you give are relevant to the scenario in question, and if you can use an example relating to legal work, so much the better.

Timing

Start making applications for training positions as soon as you possibly can. For solicitors' training contracts, this may mean submitting some applications before you have started the Graduate Diploma in Law (GDL), or while you are still at undergraduate level. Timing is essential, particularly given the two-year lead time in place at some law firms. If you want to start your training contract as early as you can, and avoid having a year or more to fill, you have to apply in good time.

Be specific

Legal employers expect you to demonstrate why you are 100% committed to them, and them alone. In reality of course, you are desperate for a training contract, and you will be making a lot of applications! The way around this is to take each application on its own, and make sure you apply afresh to every one. Avoid generalisations in your answers: don't take a good example or phrase from one application and force it into another just because it sounded good. You need to go back to a blank sheet and draft each application from scratch. Recruiters will spot any re-hashed text, and will be on the lookout for people who have taken the time to submit answers that could only apply to the questions they have asked.

Approach and tone

You are applying to professional organisations, so you must get the tone of your application right. This means using clear, professional language, and avoiding anything that is superfluous to getting your message across. Wait for a rapport to develop between you and the people you meet in the organisation before you take a less formal approach. This prevents hostages to fortune, and is an approach that will be expected of you throughout your legal career.

Open-mindedness

Wherever you end up, you will be working with various areas of law, different colleagues and clients, and on different matters. It is essential to demonstrate flexibility and open-mindedness about the role, and the desire to learn, even if you have an idea of which areas appeal to you the most. Some questions in application forms and interviews are aimed at examining your commitment to a career in law, but you are only at the start of your career at this stage. All junior lawyers are expected to work on whatever matters need their input. You need to show willingness to experience a range of work, and make sure you do not come across as being set on one or two specific areas only.

Tips on writing well-structured, targeted law CVs and covering letters

You will often be required to fill in an online application form (see below), but many employers prefer a CV and covering letter, particularly when dealing with applicants for work experience or placements. These are not always easy, and while there is a lot of help available generally, here are some tips specific to legal CVs and covering letters.

CVs

Law CVs are hard to put together in some ways, but are relatively straightforward in others. They are hard because you need to get across important information that distinguishes you from other applicants. It may be difficult to judge what is a positive thing to mention to one firm or chambers, or what may not be relevant. On the other hand, they are quite straightforward in that they need to contain only two basic categories of information: your academic qualifications, and any other relevant information about you.

Structuring a good legal CV

A good, clear structure is essential. A few elements to be included in legal CVs are listed below; using this order will help structure your CV logically:

- personal statement (optional)

- contact addresses

- educational history

- legal work experience

- other work experience

- skills

- interests and activities

- references.

Profile or personal statement

This should be no longer than one line, written in the third person, to summarise who you are and what you are looking for. This is optional: if you have more work history on your CV, one short statement may help focus the reader's attention on exactly what it is they are looking for. If you have less on your CV, it probably will not help to include a statement.

Contact addresses

Don't forget to put both a term-time address and a home address, as you may be contacted at any time.

Educational history, grades and dates

Put these in reverse chronological order, with the most recent first. Add every grade, and the dates of each exam or result you achieved. Add awards, prizes or other special points on a separate line, to give them prominence.

Legal work experience

You are applying for a job in law, so the first thing you need to show a potential employer is your awareness of working in the legal world. You then need to try to tie this to the position you are applying for. It's important to back up what you say here with examples, as we saw earlier in this chapter. Showing a range of experience is helpful, but even if you have only one or two examples to draw on, maximise these by summarising what you did, how you learned from them, and how this relates to what you are applying for.

Other work experience

You will most likely have gained some other work experience as you have progressed through school, university and beyond. This shows the reader of your CV that you are a good team worker, can apply yourself to a range of different tasks and responsibilities, have a good level of commercial awareness, and that you have been a valued employee in the past. This all counts in your favour, so don't be afraid to mention vacation jobs you may have had – this experience will show that you have some of the important non-legal skills a recruiter is looking for.

Skills

Any additional useful skills relevant to the role should be listed briefly. Languages are a definite plus, as are computer literacy (with qualifications if possible), a driving licence, and anything else you can offer that may either be useful to the role or demonstrate your abilities in other ways.

Interests and activities

The saying goes that 'all work and no play makes Jack a dull boy', and the last thing you want is for your application to look dull. Participation in anything from sports to acting, hobbies, travel, or anything else that you have an interest in is well worth adding. Very often a recruiter is looking for things that differentiate very high-quality but largely similar applications from each other. A particular extra-curricular achievement, or an unusual interest, may be just what they are looking for. This can also be very useful in interviews. If the interviewer is curious about something you are good at or enjoy, you will be able to answer questions on this with knowledge and authority, which will be very much to your advantage.

References

If you can, name two people who have specifically agreed to act as referees for you. If possible, one should be an academic contact who has known you and your work for at least a year or more. The other referee should be someone outside your studies, perhaps a previous employer, or someone in a position of responsibility who again has known you for some time. Family members should not be used as referees. It is possible to state that 'references are available on request', but this may risk making your CV look incomplete, or suggest that you have not got round to asking anyone before you sent the CV in. It's better to get this organised well in advance of any submission deadlines.

Where will your talent take you?

Hogan Lovells is one of the world's top 10 legal practices. Our global reach and exceptional breadth of practice ensures a broad, enriching experience for graduate trainees. With a spectrum of practice areas to explore, a prestigious client list and a positive, open culture, our focus is to enable trainees to become lawyers, and lawyers to become leaders.

To see how we help graduates transform ambition and potential into a world-class career, visit our website at:

www.hoganlovells.com/graduates

 Join us on Facebook

Profile: Hogan Lovells

Who we are

Hogan Lovells is a leading global law firm, with over 2,300 lawyers working in over 40 offices in Asia, Europe, Latin America, the Middle East, and the United States. Our scale and capability position us amongst the global elite of law firms, and provide our trainees with an international stage on which to develop their legal career.

Types of work

Our international strength across a wide range of practice areas gives us a strong reputation for corporate, finance, dispute resolution, government regulatory and intellectual property. This provides good training opportunities for those joining us.

Training programme

Our recruitment and training philosophy is very simple: our continued success as a firm depends on our ability to attract and retain the brightest and most able people.

We require every prospective trainee solicitor to undertake the accelerated LPC at BPP London. The course will prepare you for practice in the City.

Our two-year training contract is split into four six-month seats. As a trainee, you will move around four different practice areas during this time to gain as much experience as possible – one of your seats will be in either our corporate or finance group, and another in one of our litigation teams. You will also have the option of spending time in the second year of training on secondment to one of our international offices or to the in-house legal team of a major client.

As a trainee at Hogan Lovells, you will be offered as much responsibility as you can handle relating to client work as well as a comprehensive legal skills training programme, regular reviews and appraisals. After qualification, continuous training and development remain a priority – we enable the brightest minds to deepen their professional and business expertise throughout their career, which enhances the quality of advice we provide to clients, our reputation and your ability to make the very best of your expertise.

When and how to apply

Law students should apply over the summer after completion of their penultimate year and when they have their exams results (if applicable). Non-law students and graduates should apply in their final year from January onwards. Please see our website – www.hoganlovells.com/graduates – for all deadline dates and to apply online.

What we look for

As a consequence of the high-profile, demanding work the firm does, applicants need to have achieved excellent academic results from GCSE onwards. A good 2.i (or equivalent) is the minimum standard of degree applicants should have achieved consistently throughout their degree and as their final degree classification.

Applicants also need to be happy working in a team yet capable of, and used to, independent action. You will need to demonstrate an ability and desire for lateral thinking, be capable of close attention to detail, and be ambitious to succeed in a top law firm.

Vacation schemes and open days

We offer up to 70 vacation placements over two summer and one winter schemes. Each scheme is carefully designed to offer students the opportunity to gain exposure to life and work in a City law firm. During the two- and three-week programmes, students gain a broad insight into the work of the firm, as their time is split between three of our business areas. Students get involved in real work with real clients in much the same way as our trainees. This includes drafting, attending meetings, doing legal research and, where possible, attending court. To complement this there is a comprehensive programme of talks, workshops and social events.

Vacation scheme students are paid £300 per week. The closing date for 2012 winter vacation scheme applications is 2 November 2012. The closing date for summer vacation scheme applications is 18 January 2013. Final-year non-law students are eligible to apply for the winter vacation scheme.

We also hold open days and programmes for first-year law students throughout the academic year. Information on the dates and application deadlines for these open events can be found on our website at www.hoganlovells.com/graduates.

Case study

Sara Lynn is a trainee at Hogan Lovells International LLP who studied law at Trinity College, Dublin. Here she describes a day from her second seat in investment banking and funds litigation

8.30a.m.: I usually walk to work as it is a great way to clear my mind and get ready for the day ahead. The breakfast selection in the staff restaurant is excellent and I grab some porridge on the way to my desk.

9.15a.m.: I arrive at my desk and check my emails and calendar appointments, updating my 'to do' list and prioritising my tasks for the day. I have a quick chat with my supervisor about the emails that have come through overnight.

9.30a.m:. The case my team is working on is high profile and fast-paced. I have joined the department at an exciting stage as a trial is coming up in the next few months and I am gaining real exposure to the pre-trial stages and motions. Next week a number of applications will be heard in the commercial court and so I have been busy preparing and updating the bundles for the hearing.

10.30a.m.: I am soon ready to head off to court with the documents that came through last night. One of the best aspects of a litigation seat is the constant interaction with the court process. The learning is very 'hands-on' and never dull.

11.30a.m.: Back at my desk I check through my emails. I have received an email from Philip, a partner in my department, requiring an urgent research note on the AIM rules ahead of a client call. I pop around to see Philip and obtain more information on the task, which turns out to be relatively straightforward. The partners, and all other members of the team, are extremely approachable and there is a warm, collegiate atmosphere in the office. The research does not take long and I summarise the information in an email to Philip.

1p.m.: I head to the staff restaurant to have lunch with some other trainees.

2p.m.: Once a month I take part in the firm's Debate It programme. This is a community initiative which involves leading an after-school debating club at a local primary school. I thoroughly enjoy the sessions and it is a really rewarding way to give back to the community.

3.30p.m.: I arrive back in the office and check my emails. Philip has emailed to thank me for the note and to update me on how the call went. More bundle updates have come through and I flag the relevant emails so I can collect them all at the end of the day. I then turn to my 'to do' list.

4p.m.: Each month the department distributes a Legal and Financial Risk Newsletter to clients and the trainees usually contribute an article. This month I have been asked to draft an article on a recent case involving the interpretation of certain sections of the ISDA Master Agreement. I have been working on this for an hour or so each day this week and so settle down with a cup of tea to review and complete my article.

6p.m.: I complete my article and begin to collate the bundle updates received throughout the day. While I'm doing so I discuss the developments in the case that day with my supervisor, asking questions on procedural aspects I did not understand and discussing the case strategy.

7.15p.m.: I make sure that my supervisor does not need any more help and then head off to meet a fellow trainee for dinner. She is currently on secondment with a client of the firm and I'm keen to hear how she is getting on as I have a secondment planned in my next seat. Hogan Lovells offers secondments to the most prestigious clients and I am looking forward to the new challenge and increased responsibility.

General tips

- Make the CV easy on the eye. Make sure information is well spaced out, and use a logical structure (perhaps the order suggested above).

- Remove anything that is not absolutely relevant, and don't try to squeeze more information in using smaller fonts or narrower margins.

- Focus on quality not quantity, and try to stick to two sides if possible. You will not be expected to have so much relevant experience early on in your legal career to justify anything longer. If you have particular experience then it's OK to run into the top of a third page, but anything more than a few lines may be off-putting. It is better to focus on the relevant areas and cover them briefly, than to have your entire life story set out. Properly presented summaries of good experience will invite the reader to want to find out more from you in interview. Anything irrelevant will not help the reader, or the chances of your application leading to an interview.

There is a lot of information available on writing CVs, so, once again, take a look online, or in your college library or careers service. *You're Hired! CV* by Corinne Mills (Trotman, 2009) is a good place to start.

Covering letters

Similar rules apply to covering letters as to CVs: the contents should be clear, brief and logically structured. Elements that would be expected in a covering letter for a legal application are, in order:

- your address

- the date

- introduction

- why you are applying and what you have to offer

- practical points

- correct sign-off.

Address and date

Your address should be at the top of the letter, followed by the date. This is standard, and errors here do not look good. If you need more information on letter writing in general, there is a wealth of information online and elsewhere to help you.

Introduction

You should include one or two short sentences to introduce yourself. This may mention how you heard about the position, how you met a contact in a firm or organisation who put you in touch, or anything else that introduces you to the reader.

Why you are applying

Use only one or two paragraphs to show why you want the role, why you are the perfect candidate for it, and to point out specific experience, interests or other aspects of your CV that make you particularly suited to it. Try to go beyond mentioning academic results alone (although you should highlight any particular successes). It is impressive to show how your experience relates directly to the place you are applying to, and that you have done your research. Highlight what you have to offer to the employer, rather than the other way round. Show that you understand the role, and are very familiar with the organisation. Remember to tailor every application each time you send one off, specifying why you want to work for that particular firm or employer.

Practical points

Don't forget to mention that your CV is enclosed. It is also important to provide details of your availability for interview, or for an informal discussion. If there is anything else you feel the reader needs to know about you, add it here.

Correct sign-off

If you have used the addressee's name (which is always best), then sign off using 'Yours sincerely'. If you have been unable to find the name of the person to whom the letter is addressed, and have had to use 'Dear Sir or Madam', then you must sign off 'Yours faithfully'. This is a formality, but there is no flexibility with it. Finally, you will usually be enclosing something – your CV – so you should put the abbreviation 'Enc.' beneath your name, to indicate that there was an enclosure to the letter.

Practical tips

- Make absolutely sure that your grammar and spelling are correct. Proofreading letters and CVs two or three times is highly recommended, as is asking someone else to read them through as well.

- Always type your covering letter and CV, unless you have been specifically asked to write in longhand (some employers do request handwritten covering letters).

- Use good-quality white letter writing paper for your letter, CV and envelope. These may be tricky to fit into your printer, but it makes a good impression. Laser-printed documents look better than ink-jet.

- Print the recipient's address on the envelope if you can. Add your return address in smaller type on the front or rear.

- Don't staple anything together. If the recipient wants to do this, let them do it. This is better than requiring them to pull apart pages that are already stapled.

- Double-check that you have the correct address and postcode, and use first-class post!

Application forms

With online forms, some employers allow you simply to attach a CV and covering letter, and only require basic additional information to be submitted through a form. If you have followed the steps above, then this is a straightforward process.

Many other employers require applications to be made through a detailed online form. Online application forms are a particular favourite with the larger law firms, not least as they help with the administrative burden of processing several hundred applications, all of which are submitted around the same time. Online forms also allow the recruiting organisation to tailor questions specifically to their own requirements, increasing the likelihood that applicants' answers will be unique to that organisation.

This section of the chapter is therefore geared to those applying to these law firms, and we will use the term 'firm' here to mean any organisation that requires a form to be submitted as part of the application process for a training position. These forms can be daunting: in addition to requesting a lot of personal information from applicants, there may be five or more questions, each one requiring responses of a few hundred words. The tips below will help you tackle them.

The golden rule is that no matter how many applications you make, they must all be unique, and tailored specifically to the firm you are approaching. It is a very time-consuming process, but poor applications or covering letters are very easy to identify, and the only progress that your application is likely to make will be into the bin.

Preparation

It will come as no surprise that preparation is key to completing a successful application form. In addition to areas where you will be required to provide your educational background, grades and dates, the most important sections are the free text questions. There will usually be four or five questions, each with a text box usually allowing you a maximum of perhaps 500 words to craft your answer. They look deceptively simple, but your application will stand or fall according to your responses!

Plan your time

Plan your time properly. Find out what the closing dates are for applications, and do not miss the deadline. You must always give yourself enough time to do a draft version of each application, and as many revisions as you need, well before it has to be submitted. Deadlines for online forms are automated, and missing the deadline by just a second or two will mean that your application will not be processed. Some firms frown on applications being sent in at the last minute. They may have made a start on collating responses already, and may look at last-minute submissions as hinting at poor time management. Other firms take a different approach, and will look at all submitted applications only after the closing date, as a single batch. In this case, submitting early may be a disadvantage, if you have gained something important to add to your application since submitting it. The best advice is to make sure you know exactly what the closing date is for every application, and make sure they are all submitted about a week before the closing date.

How long should you spend on an application?

Of course, this will vary from one employer to another, but it may take the equivalent of at least one or two full working days to put together the best responses possible. Most online forms have a 'save as you go' facility. Use this to buy yourself time, and to provide some breathing space between working on applications. Resist the temptation to draft and submit an application in one sitting. If you leave it a couple of days and come back to it, you will most likely see that improvements are needed. You may be surprised at how much the application will benefit from some further improvement work, and how easy it is to spot where improvements are needed, when you look at it with fresh eyes.

Keep track

Keep a record of your progress. You will be approaching a number of different potential employers, as well as networking with many other people as you go through each stage of your application and training process. It can be hard to keep track of who you spoke to, when, and about what, as well as who you applied to, and when. If you keep a spreadsheet with a record of dates, contacts, and a note of what you did, this will be very useful to keep track of progress and help you remember who you have contacted and applied to over the months and years.

Reapply

Rejections are normal and are part of the application process. It's reasonable, and sometimes necessary, to reapply after an initial rejection, particularly if you have subsequently gained additional experience or skills – or if you are now just better at making applications than the first time. Don't go overboard though. If you can't convince a firm or chambers after two or three applications, then you have probably done all you can. At this stage it is better use of your time to broaden your search for other opportunities and potential employers.

Be persistent

It's important to keep going, and to remember that one thing that is fully within your control is keeping up with your academic work, your applications, and your work experience, all of which help develop your CV. Everything you do to build your profile will be valuable, and each added piece of experience, or good grade you achieve, contributes directly to your employability.

Practical tips for online applications

- Check your spelling and grammar. Print out your form and read it on paper. It is easier to spot errors and inconsistencies on hard copy than on the screen.

- Stick to the word limit. Use concise, short sentences. Beware of conjunctions (words that join phrases together: 'and', 'but', 'with', etc.). These add to the word count, and make one long sentence, where two shorter ones may be clearer.

- Make sure you answer the question asked. This may seem obvious, but when you are keen to put across your achievements, you may be tempted to shape your answer around the question you wanted to be asked, rather than the one that actually was.

- Use different examples to illustrate different points. If you are asked about leadership in one question, and about teamwork in another, avoid using the same example in both. Recycling may suggest that you have limited experience to draw on.

- Make absolutely sure you have not put in any silly mistakes. The ultimate crime is to put the wrong firm name into an application. This is unforgivable from the point of view of the reader, but it does happen, and occasionally errors creep in for all sorts of reasons. Before you send anything out, check and check again that nothing has slipped in that should not be there. This approach is exactly the same in legal practice, so it is a good habit to get into now.

Case study

James Evans is an associate at Lewis Silkin LLP, and tells us about the application process

When it comes to training contract applications, you do have to manage your expectations, as it is a daunting process. Rejections will almost inevitably happen time and again, and you just have to learn not to take it personally, as it is part of the process. You have to find ways around any problem spots on your CV, and be realistic. For instance, I had glandular fever during my A levels and didn't feel this situation was dealt with well by my school. My grades were A, B and C, but I could have done better. I made up for this by gaining good results at law school, and am now an associate at a City firm.

Case study

Ed Chivers is a solicitor at Farrer & Co, London

I was one of the fortunate few who did not have to go through a huge number of interviews and flood the in-trays of HR departments with my CV in order to secure a training contract. I think this was because I was realistic in the firm that I applied to and ensured that my application and CV were tailored specifically for that firm. Granted, the competition was less as I was applying to a regional firm, but there were still about 50 applicants for two training posts, so it was important to ensure that my application stood out.

It helped that I was historically from the area where the firm was based. When applying to a regional firm, this is vitally important – if you do not have links to the area then you must demonstrate a commitment to moving into the area. Regional firms do not like people who come down from London just because it's a job – they like to retain staff.

A recently qualified solicitor's opinion of the application process

'Getting a training contract or pupillage is a bit like organising a huge logistical operation, like planning D Day. You need to call in every available resource over a prolonged period of time to secure that training position. You almost need to be a bit obsessive about it, to try and find angles in everyday situations that might help you. Something you've read in the news or the legal press may crop up in an interview, or might make good material around which to shape an application response. Someone you meet may end up being a useful contact, or might know someone else who may be useful.

'And all the while, you're working away on your studies, and building your legal work experience. It's a lot to manage, but it really pays off when you finally get an offer. Plus, your suitability as a lawyer is closely related to your ability to manage all aspects of the qualification process: doing applications, studying, getting legal work experience, and all your extra-curricular stuff needed to get a really strong CV.'

How to shine at interview

Interviews are a vital part of the selection process, but it's natural to feel apprehensive about them. The role you are applying for is important, and it's a slightly artificial process to find yourself sitting in a room opposite people you have never met before, and being asked probing and often quite tricky questions. It's not an ideal way to get a dialogue going, but with good preparation, you can make interviews a genuinely two-way process, where you get to extract as much information from your potential future employer as they will from you.

Here are some hard-earned tips from lawyers who have been through the process themselves and have survived to give their insight and advice. Some come from lawyers who are involved in recruitment within their organisation, and are well placed to give some ideas about what legal employers are looking for in their trainees or pupils.

Preparation before the interview

Once you hear that you have been asked in for interview, you should go back over your application, and make sure you are completely familiar with everything you said when you applied initially. Then, think about how you would question what you are now reading. Do you have examples, or more details to back up your statements? Is anything you said particularly likely to invite questions? Going over this again will help you prepare for some of the questions that are likely to come up. Do this well in advance of the interview, and a final time a day or two before the interview day, so it's fresh in your mind.

Take some time to research the organisation again before the interview. You will have done a lot of research already, but you may benefit from a quick reminder of the firm's structure, or to get an update on what the firm has been doing recently. Are there any important new announcements or success stories on its website? Has it been mentioned in the legal press recently? Being up to speed on this will help you tackle many different kinds of questions in interview, and will give you material to draw on to back up what you say.

Make sure you know the interview process beforehand. You may have received some information on what the format of the interview will be, but, if not, you should speak to HR, or the person who contacted you about the interview. They will be able to provide information on how many people will interview you, who they are, how many interviews there will be, how long they may take, and other general information, if this has not been communicated to you already.

Assessment days

Assessment days are becoming increasingly popular among many legal recruiters. They are designed to test applicants' abilities not only in one-to-one interviews but also in terms of how they interact with each other as a group. This may be done through assessing how candidates handle different assessments and tasks, as well as through less formal activities such as social gatherings over lunch, or over drinks at the end of the day. If your interview is structured more like an assessment day, it is even more important that you know the format.

In addition to getting details of how the interviews themselves may be structured, you should also ask about any other tasks or assessments you will be required to do, to give you a chance to prepare for them. Some common exercises that interviewees may be required to do are listed below.

- **Making a presentation:** Will you be given a topic, or can you choose one? How many people will you be presenting to? Who will they be? How long should your presentation be?

- Group activities: You will be set a task to complete as a group, with specific outcomes. You will be observed during the task, and assessed on how you participate and interact with others, as well as on your material contribution to the outcome. This is the ideal time to demonstrate that you really are a good team player, and can take the lead and/or work alone when needed. Think back to past episodes of *The Apprentice* and you will be some way to seeing what works, and what doesn't!

- Written tests: These may take the form of a practical problem question, a legal case analysis, or writing a letter or memo based on a given scenario.

- Psychometric tests: These are designed to assess your suitability for the role. They can vary greatly: some are similar to personality tests, asking how you would react in certain situations. Others are reasoning exercises, which may involve reading and summarising a passage of text, or answering a number of discrete questions under strict timed conditions, to test the speed and accuracy with which you process information.

If you are unclear about what will come up on the day, ask. You need to know what to expect, if you are to be properly prepared. If you need more information or help in preparing for an interview, then speak to your careers advisers. They will be able to provide you with additional information based on experience, and can arrange invaluable practice interviews.

Interviews and assessments: dos and don'ts on the day

Do

- Dress appropriately. This means a suit and tie for men, and suit (skirt or trousers) for women. Make sure your hair is tidy and your shoes are clean. The same goes for open days and vacation schemes: don't get too comfortable and turn up in jeans on the last day, as this won't make a good impression. Let your charisma and personality shine through from what you say and do, not through what you wear.

- Bring a pen and paper. These will of course be provided for any assessments, but it may save a search or an awkward moment if you need to make a note of something such as a phone number or email address of someone you've met on the day.

- Aim to arrive about half an hour early. Don't arrive too early though, as you don't want to end up in any difficult situations, or having to wait in reception for ages. If you are very early, find somewhere round the corner to have a coffee, and go back over your application form, CV and/or covering letter.

- Ask where the interviewers want you to sit when you are called in to the interview. This is not only polite, but also shows you are happy to be positioned where they prefer. Note that with most law firms you will be interviewed in a meeting room or conference room, rather than in an individual's office.

- Be aware of any mannerisms you may have that may be off-putting or obvious to someone who doesn't know you. Be conscious of fidgeting, or other actions that might show you are nervous, and bear in mind that some mannerisms can be taken as signs of insecurity. As mentioned earlier, video-taped practice interviews with a careers adviser can help show you how you come across to others in interview situations, allowing you to make any adjustments in how you present yourself, well in advance of the real thing.

- Ask for a glass of water if you want one. This helps if you get a dry throat, and taking an occasional sip gives you time to think about an answer.

- Make sure you follow the format correctly for any exercise you are asked to do. If you are writing a letter, make sure it is addressed and signed off correctly (for example, see the information on page 184 for tips on structuring letters). If you are writing a memo, make sure you state who the memo is to, who it's from, with a date and a subject line. Use proper formatting, and bullet points for summaries.

- Expect to be pushed in an interview. Different interviewers will push you to different degrees. If you have a single interviewer, they may push a point until you can't answer it further. They are testing your ability to go to the very end of your thought process. Admitting that you just don't know the answer, or that you cannot take something any further may feel bad at the time, but if this is true, and you have shown how you have arrived at this end point, then you should not be afraid of saying it. There may be no further to go, and the interviewer will be interested in your thinking, and how you react to being right at the outer limits of your knowledge.

- Suggest possible answers that might be appropriate, if you are totally stuck as to what the correct answer might be to a question. This demonstrates that you can think around problems, and persist with tough points in a logical, well-structured way.

- Know how many people will be interviewing you. Typically it will be one or two, but you may be interviewed by a panel of three or more. Panel interviews are different to one-to-one interviews, but they are not necessarily worse. The more people you impress in the interview, the less of a sales job the interviewers have when reporting back to their colleagues to convince them to take you on. In a panel interview, there will inevitably be different levels of interaction with each interviewer. One interviewer may push you, while another may be disinterested. It is up to you to engage the attention of all the interviewers, whether they have asked you a question or not. If one is showing disinterest, get their attention with eye contact or subtle gesturing. Exactly how you do this will depend on the context of the interview, and you will need to assess the context and react accordingly.

- Ask for clarification on anything you're stuck on. This gives you time to think, and increases your chances of giving a good answer. Some interviewers will push you outside your comfort zone, and ask questions which clearly do not have a right or wrong answer. Some questions will be based around dilemmas, and will not have an 'answer' at all. A good interviewer will push you with hard questions, to assess how you react under pressure. Focus on remaining calm and composed, and continuing to give good responses as the interview progresses.

- Recognise your strengths and weaknesses. You will very likely be asked about these, and because they appear to be quite personal questions, they may be unsettling unless you are prepared. If you are asked about weaknesses, be honest, and support your answers with examples. Turn the question around by also giving reasons why a particular weakness may have positive attributes, rather than being merely a negative characteristic. Understanding that a particular trait is a shortcoming, but that you have taken steps to address it is a good way of demonstrating self-awareness and your capacity for personal development.

- Make sure you expand on your answers, to add supporting information or additional context, and to clarify your point. Very short or one-word answers are not likely to impress!

- Always bring a set of questions to ask. These must relate to the role and should not be too basic or obvious. In particular, make sure you do not ask about anything that can easily be found from the website or from recruitment materials. The questions you ask will depend on who you are speaking to. It is fine to ask a human resources officer more practical questions, such as how many training places are available, or when you may hear from the firm with results. These questions might not be appropriate for a senior fee earner, who may better be asked about their area of practice, or their wider role in the firm.

- Visit the office a few days before the interview if you can, to get to know where it is and how to plan your route on the day. If you need to drive, then make sure your car has plenty of petrol and is not likely to cause you problems, check that there is parking nearby and plan a route that minimises the risk of getting stuck in traffic.

- Remember that you are choosing them to work for, as much as they are choosing you. Make sure you ask about some of the other things going on at the firm. These could be social events, sports clubs, community work or other activities that people in the firm take part in. Staff will always be involved with more than just the day job, so make sure you find out as much as you need about all areas of the organisation.

- Keep smiling (but not too much!), stay positive, and remain professional and attentive – you're on show, and you owe it to yourself to come across as well as you can.

Don't

- Lie, or try to bluff answers. If you do not know the answer to something specific, then you should not pretend that you do, or try to wing your way through. You are likely to be found out, and this could do damage to how you are perceived. Instead, try to draw from examples of things you have done that demonstrate that you are what they are looking for. This is where your involvement in extra-curricular activities and work experience comes in. However, if you are lacking experience in a particular area and have little to draw on for a particular point in the interview, then acknowledge this. Showing that you understand why the issue is important, and that you are willing to do something to address it, is far better than trying to talk your way around it.

- Waffle in your answers. Keep to the point, and if you notice you are drifting into vague territory, take a breath and regain focus.

- Be indignant, negative or aggressive, no matter how hard you are pushed, and no matter how frustrated you may be. It may be fine to be annoyed at yourself, but not at the interviewers!

- Come across as arrogant. Respect everyone you meet, be they qualified fee earners, support staff, fellow candidates, or anyone else.

- Ask questions on difficult or technical points of law, or for the interviewer's opinion on complex legal issues. This risks putting you on the spot, and exposing the limits of your legal knowledge. General questions about areas of practice are fine and are expected, but anything really technical or oblique may make you look as if you are trying to look smarter and more informed than you actually are. You will very likely be asked for your view on the same point, and if you can't put forward anything solid, this will not look good.

- Ask about the working hours, or how often you will be expected to work late. It may be fine to mention work–life balance, but only if this is something the employer makes a point of in their literature. You should already know quite a lot about the firm's culture, and if it has a reputation for working its trainees particularly hard. Even if you don't, the interview is not the time to ask!

- Take risks by using slang, dressing casually, or being overly familiar. It takes time to get to know people, so treat the interview process with the respect it deserves. Some firms like to portray themselves as cool and forward-thinking, but an interview is not the place to find out whether your definition of cool fits theirs.

- Finally – do not forget that being called for interview means that you have the potential to succeed. The organisation would not be investing time and energy with you if you had not already shown them that you are worth meeting. This is a great achievement in itself, so build on this in the interview, and show them that you are who they are looking for.

Some of these things may seem obvious, but they are all important if you are to portray yourself as favourably as you can. There is a lot of crossover between preparing for an interview and preparing for work in your future legal career. Both involve important skills for all lawyers, and you need to be able to demonstrate that you understand the significance of good preparation and appropriate presentation the very first time you meet your potential employer.

Want a career that's everything you expected?

Apply elsewhere

You'll have noticed, it's a changing world. Everywhere, new business models are emerging Increasingly, size and reputation alone aren't enough – clients are more swayed by insight, flexibility and value. In ten years' time, the landscape for commercial law firms is going to look very different indeed.

Why not help shape it?

www.pinsentmasons.com/graduate

Pinsent Masons

Profile: Pinsent Masons LLP

Pinsent Masons is a full service international law firm with over 2,500 staff globally. We have offices in all the major UK business centres and more recently have been developing our overseas network of offices in Europe and the Asia Pacific and Gulf regions.

Pinsent Masons provides legal services to a wide variety of clients including multinational corporations, government departments and public sector institutions. Pinsent Masons has an ambitious strategy for growth in the years ahead. Our London office will be stronger, our international reach will be greater, but our values will remain the same. Anyone looking to join the firm will need to buy into this vision.

To achieve the above we need exceptional individuals. This is not about the school or university you attended but your unique qualities as an individual. To be successful you will need to possess excellent analytical and problem-solving skills, have the ability to develop strong working relationships with both clients and colleagues, and finally you must have a genuine interest in our clients and the business world.

Vacation placement

A vacation placement is the ideal way to demonstrate you have the ability to be a successful commercial lawyer. By taking part you will get a 'real' appreciation of our firm, culture, people and the opportunities available. You can test drive a career with Pinsent Masons, experience the energy and dynamism of our teams and have a first-hand look at some of the work we do.

On the placement you will work alongside trainees and solicitors on real client matters, learn about the different practice areas within the firm and get to know as many of our people as possible. At the same time a vacation placement offers you the chance to demonstrate your suitability for a training contract through your appetite for work and responsibility and your business sense. Indeed, a majority of our trainee solicitors have completed a placement at the firm.

To find out more, visit our website (www.pinsentmasons.com/graduate), or alternatively you may like to read about the experience of former vacation placement students by visiting www.ratemyplacement.co.uk.

Training contract

Alternatively, you can apply directly for a training contract outside the vacation placement programme where you will be assessed at one of our assessment centres across the UK. This route can be more suitable for candidates who either are already in full-time employment or have previous legal work experience.

Either way, we welcome applications from both law and non-law students and graduates. While numbers can fluctuate from year to year, we typically recruit around 80 trainee solicitors each year across our UK offices.

Questions likely to come up in written applications and/or interviews

These are your opportunity to demonstrate that you have the skills and competencies the recruiter is looking for. There are limitless possible questions that might crop up. Here are some that are known to have been asked in training contract and pupillage interviews, to give you an idea of what you might expect.

Questions can usually be divided into five general areas.

1. Questions relating to how you view your career.

2. Questions relating to law.

3. Questions relating to your skills and competencies.

4. Questions relating to commercial awareness.

5. Questions designed to test your ability to deal with unexpected or tricky issues.

Questions relating to your career

- Why law? Why do you want to be a solicitor/barrister?

- Where do you see yourself in five years' time?

- Where else have you applied?

- What are you expecting to gain from a career in law?

- What qualities are needed to be a good solicitor/barrister? Do you have these?

- Explain how your (legal or other) experience applies to our work.

You should be prepared to answer questions on your career in some detail, and with conviction. You need to be able to show that your decisions are logical, and based on good information and experience.

Questions relating to law

- Why have you applied to this firm/set?

- What differentiates us from our competitors?

- What has been the most important development in an area of law we work in, and why?

- Give an example of a recent decision that you agree/disagree with, and explain your position.

These can often be fairly self-explanatory questions with no hidden traps. They are, however, central to your application. You are applying for a legal role, so you have to be strong on the legal aspects of the job. You won't be expected to be an expert, but you should be able to answer law-related questions convincingly, based on up-to-date information.

You need to be able to demonstrate why you chose the firm, chambers or organisation interviewing you, and why you are particularly suited to it. Go back over the tips earlier in this chapter on page 176. You need to demonstrate the same points at interview as you do in applications.

Expect questions on current developments in the commercial and legal world, and anything in the news that concerns the areas of law you are interested in and that relate to the position you are applying for. Think carefully about how areas of law may cross over. For example, if a news story breaks about financial wrongdoing, is this only a criminal investigation? Which other authorities might be involved? What about other aspects, such as directors' obligations, or how shareholders might be affected? What about reputation management, or any number of other issues that might come into play? Showing that you understand the relationship between the law and the commercial, everyday implications of its application will be looked on very favourably.

Questions relating to your skills and competencies

- Are you better working alone, or as part of a team?

- Give an example of a time you experienced conflict or disagreement. How did you resolve this?

- Give an example of your ability to negotiate and persuade. How did you go about this, and how successful were you?

- What is your greatest strength, and your greatest weakness? How do these help/hinder your work, and what are you doing about them?

- Give an example of a problem you solved. Explain your approach, and what you would do differently if faced with the same problem again.

- What achievement are you most proud of?

- What is the biggest mistake you have ever made?

- How do you deal with failure?

- How do your friends describe you?

- Why are you a good person to have on a team?

- What makes you the ideal candidate for the role?

You may be asked any number of standard questions about yourself, but you will not be expected to repeat what is on your CV or application form. There may be a particular point of interest in something you have mentioned, which may be explored in detail. Otherwise, be prepared to answer questions such as these clearly and positively.

Questions relating to commercial awareness

Commercial interview questions are intended to assess your ability to identify the key commercial considerations that a typical business will need to think about. From the answers you give, the interviewer will assess your suitability as a potential legal adviser to commercial clients. Your answers therefore need to demonstrate both commercial sense and common sense. There will most likely not be a right or wrong answer to these questions, but some points should usually be considered in most answers, such as:

- supply and demand

- competition

- pricing

- regulatory issues

- location, premises and leases

- branding and identity

- marketing and advertising

- company structure (independent company, partnership, franchise?)

- staff.

Further aspects that you can think of, which may be relevant to the question, include consideration of potential disputes or problems that might be faced, and how they may be resolved.

Some recent examples of commercially focused questions asked at interview are given below.

- Explain how the 2008 recession came about, and what you would expect its effects to have been on us as a firm/set. What might be done to minimise any negative effects? Might there have been any positive effects?

- You are about to set up a coffee shop next door. How would you go about doing this?

Commercial awareness can sometimes appear to be a concept that is shrouded in mystery. However, it is nothing more than having good practical knowledge of how businesses operate, coupled with a good understanding of current issues affecting the business world. Look back at 'Commercial awareness' in Chapter 8 for ideas on improving your general commercial awareness, if necessary.

Questions designed to test your ability to deal with unexpected or tricky issues

These can be very varied, ranging from 'dinner party' style questions, to problems and dilemmas, or may just be questions designed to find out more about you as a person.

- With which three historical figures (living or dead) would you most like to have a dinner party, and why?

- How long is the London Tube network?

- What do you do in your spare time?

- You are in a client meeting with a supervisor who is giving incorrect advice. What do you do?

- If you knew you were about to be stranded on a desert island for a year, which five things would you most want to have with you, and why?

These questions do not fit easily in the other categories, but your answers may be quite revealing about you as a person. They may be totally off the wall, or centred around a dilemma, to test clarity of thought, processes of reasoning and ability to present a coherent analysis of the problem.

Summary

The tips above should be helpful in getting you through the door, and securing that elusive training position. If all goes to plan, you still have some work ahead of you, to get to qualification and beyond, but by the time you have your training contract or pupillage in place, you're almost there. Congratulations!

PART 4
Alternative routes and career options

12

Alternative careers with a legal qualification

Many people come to law with the intention of progressing through each stage of qualification necessary to become a solicitor or barrister. However, not everyone makes it all the way to full qualification. There are many reasons for this, and it is a myth that not going all the way to full qualification is in some way a failure.

Regardless of the level of legal qualification you have, all are valuable and relevant to your professional life. Your legal studies and work experience may also have introduced you to areas of work and possible career options that you might not have come across otherwise, and legal work experience will equip you with skills that apply to other areas as much as they do to law.

Very often there are forces at work beyond your control that influence how things work out, the most obvious being the ongoing effects of the recent economic downturn. Training opportunities have been significantly reduced, lawyers have been made redundant, and newly qualified solicitors and barristers are finding it hard going to secure a job at the end of their training. There has been no change to the calibre of candidates coming through the system, but the professional and economic environment has become more difficult, and many able candidates have found themselves in a position they could not have expected just a few years previously. Things are getting better, however, and trainee solicitor retention rates are back on the increase, while recent figures from the Bar Council show the number of qualified barristers to have increased steadily between 2005 and 2010.

As with any competitive area, you will experience rejections as your career progresses. It can be almost impossible to react positively to a rejection, particularly when you know you have done all you can, but sometimes things happen that are out of your hands. The important thing is to accept a knock-back as part of the process, and keep going. Each rejection may be an opportunity to reconsider the direction you had planned for your career. Even if your route needs to be adjusted along the way, this doesn't mean you will end up with a career any less worthwhile than you initially intended.

Remember that experience is what sets you apart from your competitors. Continue to gain relevant experience, and this will make you increasingly employable. There is nothing to stop you working in a part-qualified role in a particular area of law, and gaining qualifications specific to that area. You can always go back to studying for the additional solicitors' or barristers' qualifications later, or you may feel this is no longer necessary if you have found an area that suits you.

In addition to technical legal knowledge, your legal qualifications provide you with a number of key skills, which all employers will be looking for.

- You are experienced in structuring reasoned arguments, and in making objective judgements and solving problems.

- You are well practised in identifying key issues in any given scenario, applying rules and other considerations, and forming conclusions and recommendations.

- You have proven ability in organising your time, managing a diverse workload, developing your own schedule and working to fixed deadlines.

- Your research skills can be applied to almost any situation requiring the analysis of large amounts of written or other material.

- You have developed good communication skills, both orally and in writing.

- You have shown that you are self-motivated, with the various course elements demonstrating your ability to work independently or as part of a group.

You may be yet to secure a training contract or pupillage, or you may have decided that going all the way to full qualification as a solicitor or barrister is not for you. If things haven't worked out at a particular stage of the qualification process, then you can always come back to law through another route later. Remember that the Academic Stage qualifications are valid for seven years, during which time you can go on to the Legal Practice Course (LPC) or Bar Professional Training Course (BPTC). Barristers must start their pupillage within five years of the BPTC or BVC, while for future solicitors, the LPC is valid indefinitely.

Plenty of alternative careers options exist for people at all levels of legal qualification, and some suggestions are set out below.

Alternative careers where legal qualifications are seen as a distinct advantage

We looked at some of the different careers available to part-qualified lawyers or those looking for experience in specific areas of law in Chapter 5. There are many more options available too. Many recruiters will view a law degree or other legal qualification very positively: the law will always apply in various ways to any area you work in, although some are more closely regulated or more focused on specific areas of law than others, and in these areas your legal skills will be especially useful.

Speak to your careers advisers for ideas, and keep up your research. Meanwhile, here are some alternative areas in which legal qualifications are viewed favourably. They are arranged alphabetically.

Accountancy and tax consultancy

Chartered accountants advise on financial aspects of their clients' business, in order to improve performance and financial management, in accordance with law and regulation. They work in a wide variety of different areas, including commerce and industry, government, and the public sector. Areas of work include financial reporting, tax advice, carrying out or managing audits, corporate finance, insolvency, and management of accounting processes and systems.

There is considerable crossover between areas of accountancy and areas of law, given the extent to which tax and financial regulation are central to both professions. Any legal qualification is extremely useful to an accountant; indeed, some of the professional accountants' qualifications include a legal element, and vice versa. Further, since many accountancy firms are structured in a similar way to law firms, skills picked up through work experience in a law firm will be applicable in an accountants' practice.

Useful experience relevant to this area:

- LPC and BPTC commercial, business and tax modules

- electives in any area of finance or commercial law.

Barristers' clerk

Barristers' clerks manage all administrative aspects of a barrister's practice, acting as practice managers. They take responsibility for liaising with instructing solicitors, selecting and booking out suitable barristers for the kinds of matters that are coming in, organising timetabling of court hearings, conferences and other work, and managing financial aspects of the practice, such as collecting fees and managing budgets. They need to be familiar with court procedures and developments in areas of law relevant to the barristers they work with, and while clerks are not required to be legally qualified, legal experience is an advantage given the nature of the work.

Useful experience relevant to this area:

- any legal qualifications

- interest in litigation, court work and dispute resolution

- work experience in a barrister's chambers or litigation/contentious department of a solicitors' firm.

Business consultancy work

A solid grounding in the legal foundation subjects and practical knowledge of business and commercial law are useful in any commercial context. Consultancy work offers the opportunity to be involved in a wide variety of projects, in whichever areas interest you. You are your own boss – you can choose what you work on, how and when you work, and you can take on a lot of direct responsibility.

Useful experience relevant to this area:

- LPC and BPTC business law modules and commercially focused electives

- work experience in a law firm or barristers' chambers, operating in relevant commercial areas.

A warning on working freelance

If you decide to work freelance in areas that may make use of your legal knowledge, you need to be aware of the types of work you are, and are not, eligible to do. Some legal work is 'reserved' for qualified solicitors only, requiring particular qualifications and professional indemnity insurance. These include certain kinds of court and litigation work, as well as probate and notarial work (see Chapter 5 for more details on these). There are complex rules governing this, and you need to make absolutely sure you are operating within your levels of competence. You may not come across these areas in some commercial work, but it is essential that you understand what kinds of work you may or may not do. It is your responsibility to ensure that you know your limitations: check with the Solicitors Regulation Authority (SRA) or Bar Standards Board (BSB) for more information.

Chartered surveyor, chartered loss adjuster and insurance work

A huge amount of legal work is generated through the insurance industry, as claims are pursued following events that have resulted in loss or damage to insured parties. Familiarity with the legal foundation subjects of contract and tort, as well as any litigation experience is a distinct advantage for working in the insurance industry. The role of a chartered surveyor is to assess the value of an asset, and to provide a report giving an objective assessment of its value, and any defects or points to note, for a prospective purchaser, insurer or lender. If loss or damage occurs to an asset and an insurance claim is made, then a chartered loss adjuster will investigate the circumstances and causes of the loss, and will inspect the damaged asset, if this is possible. They will provide a written report to the insurer as to the merits of any insurance claim made, and the value of reinstatement or payment that should be made.

Useful experience relevant to this area:

- any legal qualifications

- interest or experience in litigation

- general commercial work experience.

Citizens Advice Bureau and Law Centre work

These are free, impartial services offered to people to help with legal, financial or other problems. The Citizens Advice Bureau (CAB) offers free face-to-face advisory services and services by phone and email to help people with their day-to-day legal problems. The CAB is also actively involved in shaping government policy and legislation. In addition to assisting with advisory work, opportunities exist within the CAB in areas such as lobbying, media relations, training and information management.

Law Centres assist individuals with access to legal support, as well as performing a number of more policy-driven areas of work, such as taking on test cases, providing education and training services in specific areas of law, working with and providing legal services for public services and the community, and lobbying for changes in the law for the public benefit.

There are very few paid positions available, with solicitors, barristers and other staff usually offering their time voluntarily. CAB and Law Centre work is interesting and rewarding, giving excellent experience of advising clients in real-life situations. It also offers the opportunity to make a real difference to people's lives.

Useful experience relevant to this area:

- LPC and BPTC advocacy modules

- experience in litigation and advocacy in a law firm or with a barrister

- experience representing clients through pro bono or Law Centre work

- particular interest or experience in human rights, public and administrative law.

Civil Service

The Civil Service supports the government in providing advisory and other services to assist the government in implementing its policies. Its main departments are the Department for Work and Pensions, the Ministry of Defence, HM Revenue and Customs, and the Ministry of Justice, which together span a vast range of activities. Lawyers are involved in all departments, and there are good career development prospects for graduates. The Civil Service Fast Stream programme exists to encourage talented graduates to apply to the service, and offers access to senior-level experience (including legal experience) in a relatively short time frame, enabling rapid promotion for quality candidates. The 'streams' cover five areas: analysis and economics, human resources, technology in business, European institution work, and work in Northern Ireland. Legal experience is useful in almost any role within the Civil Service, not only within legal departments.

Useful experience relevant to this area:

- Graduate Diploma in Law (GDL), LPC or BPTC

- particular interest or experience in human rights, public and administrative law, European and international law.

Company secretary

Company secretaries perform important administrative duties, such as ensuring that documents and forms are filed at Companies House, signing off company accounts, chairing board meetings and drafting minutes. Company secretaries are mandatory for public companies, but it has not been a legal requirement for private limited companies to have a company secretary since April 2008. Many private limited companies have kept their company secretaries on, however, as a dedicated staff member to keep on top of the company's corporate administrative work, and to be an important point of contact between management, shareholders and other parties with an interest in the performance of the company.

Useful experience relevant to this area:

- LPC and BPTC business law modules

- work experience in a law firm's corporate or commercial departments

- work experience assisting senior management of a company or other organisation.

Foreign and Commonwealth Office work

The Foreign and Commonwealth Office (FCO), or Foreign Office, is the UK's international diplomatic service, supporting the British government and its citizens overseas. The FCO's objective is to maintain and advance Britain's influence in the international community, and to develop foreign policy in areas such as countering terrorism, preventing and resolving conflict, promoting economic growth, and developing effective international institutions. The FCO's work is dynamic and constantly adapting to international developments, and is interesting and rewarding. Work experience and placement schemes exist to give an insight into the work and culture of the service.

Useful experience relevant to this area:

- any legal qualifications or experience in the commercial or public sectors

- particular interest or experience in human rights, public and administrative law, European and international law.

HM Revenue and Customs

HM Revenue and Customs (HMRC) is the central authority managing tax and customs and other central financial administration for the UK. Lawyers play a key role at HMRC in all areas of tax and finance matters, including advising government departments on policy, human rights, European and international law, as well as conducting litigation on HMRC's behalf to recover tax. Legal training opportunities exist within HMRC, and given the fundamental role and broad range of work, HMRC offers some of the best legal experience and training available in tax and related areas of law.

Useful experience relevant to this area:

- LPC and BPTC commercial, business and tax modules

- electives in any area of finance or commercial law

- interest or experience in contentious or non-contentious work

- interest in financial or tax-related work.

Human resources and recruitment

The effective management of staff within an organisation often requires a dedicated human resources (HR) manager or team. Working in HR puts you at the heart of your employer's business, and will require a good working knowledge of the business, its management, strategy and direction, as well as its people. Some of the main areas of HR work include recruiting and retaining staff, identifying and solving staff-related problems, and managing staff procedures and training. Legally qualified HR staff are particularly valuable to many employers, including legal organisations, as employment law is constantly updated and an understanding of key legal principles is essential. The larger legal employers often look for legally qualified HR staff; working in HR in a law firm may be a good opportunity to build and develop your knowledge of employment law as well as your practical experience. Many of the larger legal recruitment consultancies look for legally qualified candidates when recruiting their own staff. This is a very popular route to take for those with legal qualifications.

Useful experience relevant to this area:

- employment law LPC or BPTC elective

- work experience in a law firm's employment, corporate or commercial departments

- other general commercial experience.

Investment banking, finance and insurance

Investment bankers are specialists in financial services, facilitating corporate mergers of companies, acquisitions of one or more companies by another, arranging loan facilities for large corporate or government clients, or dealing with the Stock Exchange on share issues.

Specific areas of work may include business analysis or trade and project finance, in the context of either commercial or private banking services. As with accountancy, the finance industry is subject to considerable regulation by law, and is regulated by the Financial Services Authority (FSA). Many of the FSA rules and regulations are familiar to lawyers, as the rules make up an important part of legal training and practice, particularly in areas such as prevention of money laundering. Since legal qualifications and banking are closely compatible, some employers in the banking sector will view legal qualifications as a very positive attribute on a CV.

Useful experience relevant to this area:

- LPC and BPTC commercial, business and tax modules

- electives in any area of finance, banking or commercial law.

Legal library work

If you are interested in the more academic or technical aspects of law, legal information and knowledge management, then library work may be an area to consider. Most of the larger law firms have extensive law libraries, as do barristers' chambers, universities and some of the professional regulatory bodies. Librarians are not merely tasked with organising legal information and resources, but provide updates on developments in the law, put together training materials, respond to questions on specific points of law, and carry out general legal research. Law firm librarians work with colleagues across the firm, and interact with suppliers of law materials, IT and other information-related services.

Useful experience relevant to this area:

- law degree or conversion

- LPC or BPTC legal research modules

- any work experience involving legal research in a law firm or barristers' chambers.

Legal publishing and research, journalism and court reporting

There are a number of legal reference resources that are used across the profession, and which operate both online and in traditional print media. This is a growing area, as lawyers and commentators demand ever quicker and more flexible access to the latest available information. Qualified and part-qualified lawyers are often employed by legal publishers (e.g. Westlaw, LexisNexis, Practical Law Company) as staff writers and researchers to ensure that published material is relevant and accurate. Similarly, legal qualifications can be put to good use in journalism, either in the specialist legal press or elsewhere. Court reporting may also be an option: court reporters take a verbatim shorthand note of certain court proceedings, for publication as court reports.

Useful experience relevant to this area:

- all GDL, LPC and BPTC written modules and research tasks

- any experience writing articles, training materials or other documents

- any work experience involving legal research

- court and litigation experience.

Legal secretarial work

Legal secretaries play an important role assisting lawyers in all areas of legal practice, working in law firms and barristers' chambers, local authorities and courts.

Legal secretarial work can be challenging and fast-paced, perhaps assisting at court hearings, assisting with interviewing clients, researching points of law, and drafting legal documents, letters or forms. Salaries will vary according to location and experience, and employers frequently pay for legal secretaries to gain additional qualifications relevant to the legal work they do, adding to their skill set and enhancing their career prospects.

Useful experience and training relevant to this area:

- Legal Secretaries Diploma course

- work experience or temping in a law firm, chambers or court

- non-legal work experience in a professional, office-based environment

- secretarial or administrative experience.

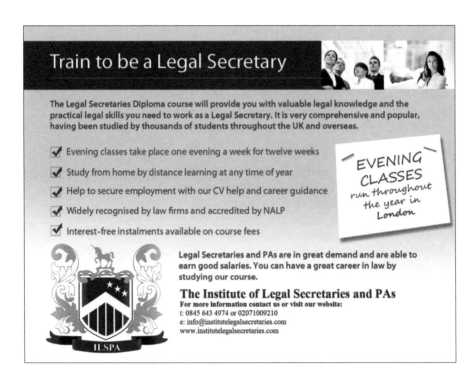

Case study

Have you considered a career as a legal secretary?

The role of a legal secretary is varied, challenging and interesting. It can be an excellent starting point for a career in law and there is great opportunity for career advancement. If you think it could be the career for you, there is an excellent course available to help you gain the valuable legal knowledge and practical skills you need to become a successful legal secretary. Moushka Dickens, from London, took the Legal Secretaries Diploma course through the Institute of Legal Secretaries and PAs and she has only positive things to say about the Institute, her studies and her new job:

'I cannot praise Amanda Hamilton enough for help, advice and for being an amazing and inspirational tutor. She has a natural gift for teaching and for instilling in others the importance and precision of studying a very detailed and complex subject which spans many different topics in law. She managed to make lessons not only very interesting but also amusing. I have found the Institute of Legal Secretaries and PAs to be very helpful when I have either telephoned or emailed them with queries regarding the course. I would recommend both the Institute and Amanda Hamilton highly to any potential students, and indeed employers.'

Moushka achieved her goal and secured a position as a legal secretary/receptionist at a law firm in Wimbledon. Moushka tells us about her new career:

'I'm being trained on the job and the work is very varied and interesting – mostly probate, matrimonial, conveyancing and immigration. I must say that I felt really confident starting this role knowing that I had been fully trained by the Institute of Legal Secretaries and PAs and I have my file ready to refer to if need be. Everything I covered in my course is all here at my job. It's great to finally be able to put into practice what I've learned and the course folder and assignments have been invaluable to me in this respect. I have had feedback that my new employers and colleagues are very pleased and impressed with my work, which is nice to know. I am enjoying my new career so far and I hope to take it further in the future. I cannot recommend the Institute of Legal Secretaries and PAs and the course highly enough for anyone who is thinking of retraining.'

The Legal Secretaries Diploma course is recognised by law firms throughout the UK. It is valued for its comprehensive content which enables people to be competent legal secretaries. Many law firms enrol their staff on to the course to gain the legal knowledge and practical skills they need.

To find out more, visit www.institutelegalsecretaries.com.

Local government

Local government (county councils and district councils) employ around 2 million people in the UK, managing public services including healthcare, property and housing, education and transport. Lawyers assist local government in a very wide range of areas, and opportunities exist for part-qualified lawyers as well as for qualified solicitors and barristers. Certain departments within councils may offer roles that are particularly well suited to those with legal experience or qualifications, such as building and planning departments, environmental services, and those departments dealing with issues involving community officers and the police.

Useful experience relevant to this area:

- GDL, LPC or BPTC

- any work experience in legal practice

- particular interest or experience in public and administrative law, human rights, including freedom of information, and community-focused work.

Management consultancy

Management consultants offer expert advice to assist organisations in optimising performance, helping to improve profitability, or assisting with specific projects that require specialist management input. The work can relate to any commercial sector and tends to be project-based, focusing on strategy, general management and HR, or operational issues such as supply chain management and information technology. The broad scope of potential areas of management consultancy work often means that several potential legal issues may apply to any given situation. A legal background is useful in identifying and understanding the implications of these issues, in order to manage them appropriately.

Useful experience relevant to this area:

- any legal qualification

- LPC or BPTC electives in business and commercial law

- work experience gained in a law firm, barristers' chambers or in-house.

Mediation and dispute resolution

Mediation is a form of alternative dispute resolution. It allows parties to a dispute to reach settlement confidentially and under their own terms, with no formal adjudication taking place. Mediation is voluntary, but is actively encouraged by the courts to run alongside formal litigation, as resolution can often be reached this way without the time and expense of going all the way to court or tribunal. The role of the mediator is to act as an impartial go-between for both parties to the dispute, assisting with drafting terms to any mediated agreement or settlement, and coordinating logistical aspects of a mediation. More information is available from the Centre for Effective Dispute Resolution (CEDR; www.cedr.com).

Useful experience relevant to this area:

- **any legal qualifications**

- **interest or experience in litigation and dispute resolution**

- **experience working with clients, perhaps through pro bono or Law Centre work.**

Parliamentary clerk

A parliamentary clerk is a skilled administrator working within the House of Commons (the 'House'), similar to a civil servant. They work in a central capacity, assisting all areas of the House, and are not affiliated to a political party. The work may involve assisting parliamentary committees with meetings and debates, preparing briefings, writing summaries and reports on positions and policies of parliamentary committees, or drafting proposed amendments to parliamentary bills. Alternatively, a parliamentary clerk may be involved in procedural work within the House, which may include drafting summaries of the day's votes and other activities, or more specialist research on policy or procedure. Positions rotate every two years, giving parliamentary clerks insight into many aspects of the workings of government. The nature of the work means that many parliamentary clerks have undergraduate or higher degrees in law or other subjects, and many have previous legal experience.

Useful experience relevant to this area:

- GDL, LPC or BPTC

- particular interest or experience in politics, human rights, public and administrative law.

Police and criminal investigative work

Working for the police offers opportunities at different levels, including joining the force as a police officer, community support officer or in any number of different support roles, including analytical support. Certain forces, including the City of London, have specialist teams tackling criminal activity specific to their location, such as economic crime or counter-terrorism activities. Experience gained through legal work or qualifications can be directly applicable in roles within many police departments.

Useful experience relevant to this area:

- GDL, LPC or BPTC modules in criminal law, public and administrative law, criminal litigation and advocacy

- particular interest in community work, helping others and combating crime.

Teaching and lecturing

Opportunities for teaching law are open to people at differing stages of qualification, with the expertise of qualified solicitors or barristers being particularly valued by colleges and universities. It is easy to envisage the kind of work this entails – take any course you have studied, and picture yourself being the person at the front of the room!

Useful experience relevant to this area:

- any legal qualifications

- any work experience in legal practice and/or teaching

- experience in advocacy, presenting and management.

Tribunal advocacy

Tribunals are similar to courts, in that cases are heard before a panel of adjudicators who decide on their outcome. They deal with specific areas of law, such as employment law, but are somewhat less formal than courts. They are intended to broaden access to dispute resolution, and to keep costs down, through allowing people either to represent themselves more easily than in court, or to choose people other than barristers to represent them (although frequently barristers are instructed in tribunal cases).

A key point of difference between some tribunals and the courts is that you do not always need special qualifications, or Higher Rights of Audience, to represent clients in tribunals (although clearly legal experience is a major advantage). Tribunal advocacy offers a combination of areas of work done by both solicitors and barristers, and is ideal for those with a keen interest in the sectors covered by the tribunal system and who are looking for contentious work involving case and document preparation and negotiation, as well as the advocacy itself.

Useful experience relevant to this area:

- LPC and BPTC advocacy modules

- experience in litigation and advocacy in a law firm or with a barrister

- experience representing clients through pro bono or Law Centre work.

13

What to do if things don't go to plan

What if . . .

. . . you don't get into law school?

Most course providers require applicants for the Graduate Diploma in Law (GDL) to have obtained at least a 2.i in their first degree. If you do not meet this requirement, and feel that your degree result does not fairly or accurately reflect your performance or potential, then discuss this with the course provider. They can give you feedback on your individual circumstances which will help you decide which direction to take. Look again at Chapter 6 for more information on formulating a strategy.

If you do not manage to get a place, then a number of alternative routes to qualification are still available, and you will still be able to gain legal work experience that will count towards formal qualification, or to strengthen your legal CV. Options that will be open to you include training through the Chartered Institute of Legal Executives (CILEx), qualifying as a registered conveyancer, or building your experience and contacts through paralegal work. See earlier chapters for more information on these.

... you don't get strong grades on the GDL, LPC or BPTC?

Strictly speaking, you are usually only required to gain a 'pass' on each of these courses, and there is no formal requirement to get a commendation or distinction in order to progress from one stage to the next, and then go on to your training contract or pupillage. The courses are not easy, and the number of assessments and exams involved means that sometimes things don't quite go to plan.

Most course providers allow you a number of retakes for certain exams or assessments, and you should check with your course provider for precise details. This will give you the opportunity to get back on track, but retakes may affect your ability to be awarded a commendation or distinction, even if you have achieved the required grades in other areas. If you are ill during exam time, then you should let your course provider know immediately, so you can plan how to progress. You may be able to sit the exams at a later time.

If you have a training contract, pupillage or other arrangement in place, you should be fully aware of any terms or conditions in the agreement with your employer which require you to achieve certain grades or standards. This is particularly important if your employer is covering any part of your course fees. Some solicitors' firms will disqualify trainees if they do not achieve certain standards in all exams and assessments throughout the law degree or conversion. You should of course be aiming high anyway, but make sure you know exactly what is expected of you. If you are having difficulties during a course, make sure you discuss this with your employer, as well as with your tutors and/or careers advisers.

If your results are patchy, then make sure you highlight the positive results in applications and interviews. The chances are that you have performed well in areas that you find interesting, and in which you might want to work, so shape your applications around these successes. If you are asked in interview about areas where you did not perform quite so well, be honest – not everyone can be an expert in every area of such a broad range of subject matter. If you were involved in relevant activities or work experience outside your studies, then this is a good thing. Highlight this, as time spent gaining broader, practical insight into areas of law that interest you might be fair justification for a blip in your academic results.

. . . you don't get a training contract or pupillage?

The truth is that there are not enough places for all candidates, but this should not put you off applying. All employers are looking for good people, and the vacancies are out there. If you have the qualifications required, and show initiative and drive, this will separate you from the competition, and you are likely to succeed.

You may need to refine your criteria as your search for a position continues, and you may need to broaden your scope to include potential employers that you did not target first time round. You may also have to look in a wider geographical area to the one you first had in mind. Revisit Chapter 11, speak to your tutors and contacts, and readjust where and how you are applying, in light of their feedback.

Sometimes you need to apply to the same employer a couple of times. You might not have had the right level of experience first time, or you may not have put in the best application, particularly if you had to apply before starting your conversion degree. You won't be discriminated against for this, but it is much easier to show yourself off as a committed candidate if you have some legal experience, academic or practical, to draw on.

You may need to leave it a year or two to gain extra skills and experience before you continue with your applications. Firms and chambers do remember applicants, and it can make a very positive impression if you take any comments you received first time, build on them, and reapply later with exactly what they are looking for.

You will need to be flexible, and to use your common sense, but if you keep trying, you will find that persistence does pay. Concentrate on gaining skills and experience, and improving your applications. Applying year after year with nothing additional on your CV is not the way to go.

If it really is not working out, then look into the other career options covered in Chapter 12. Continue to build your legal work experience, and stay on the lookout for vacancies and new avenues to pursue. You will hear about opportunities as much by word of mouth as through your own research, so keep in touch with your contacts, and don't rely solely on internet searches and advertised vacancies.

. . . you decide at any point that, after making the investment, law just isn't for you?

As with a lot of other things in life, there is no substitute for first-hand experience, and this is certainly the case with legal work. It is quite common for people to find that their expectations of what a legal career would entail are not matched by the reality of studying or working in law. Some law students find their law degree or GDL very interesting, only to find during the LPC or BPTC that they are not drawn to the practical realities of working in law. Others enjoy the academic side but find that legal work in practice is perhaps not as interesting as a career somewhere else. Others find certain elements of law interesting, and do not want to spend the time and money getting qualifications in areas broader than those they need for their particular specialist area. There may be fewer career possibilities available at a particular time in certain areas of law than you had hoped, which might force you to rethink where you are heading at any point in your legal career.

If after gaining any legal qualification you decide that a career in law isn't for you, this does not mean your experience is wasted. Everything you have learned can be applied to a huge number of other areas, and your skills will place you at a distinct advantage in the jobs market. The areas detailed in Chapter 12 are just a start – tailor your research to your areas of interest, and you will find many more.

14

Overseas applicants

Overseas applicants are subject to complex immigration rules, which have a tendency to change frequently. If you are applying to study in the UK from overseas, you need to research the UK immigration authority rules as they apply to your country. Here is a basic overview of some of the issues you may face, but it is not possible to give more than a summary here. Use this as a starting point, and do your own research to find out what applies to you.

For complete and up-to-date information on the immigration rules that apply to overseas graduate students wishing to study in the UK, consult the section for adult students on the Home Office UK Border Agency website (www.ukba.homeoffice.gov.uk/visas-immigration/studying/adult-students/).

Further useful information for overseas students on all aspects of studying in the UK is available from the UK Council for International Student Affairs (www.ukcisa.org.uk).

Are you eligible to study and/or work in the UK?

Immigration rules

The immigration rules for students currently fall under the Home Office's points-based immigration system or PBS. The rules set out three key requirements for overseas students wishing to study in the UK.

- **You are required to study at a college or university that has a PBS sponsor licence.**

- **The course you wish to study must be at a high enough academic level.**

- **You must be able to support yourself financially, and satisfy strict financial criteria.**

Most of the major law course providers are licensed PBS sponsors. The postgraduate level of the law courses required for qualification in England and Wales are at a high enough academic level also to qualify. The first two requirements are therefore likely to be satisfied in most cases for students looking to study the GDL, LPC or BPTC.

Financial points

For the third requirement, it is up to you to ensure that you satisfy the financial criteria set out in the Home Office rules. To give you an idea of the figures involved, the rules stated that in 2011, students studying in London for a course of nine months or longer needed an absolute minimum of £1,000 per month of study, plus course fees. Students studying outside London needed £5,400 plus course fees.

Note that assistance with fees may be available to students domiciled in the UK, but may not be available to some overseas students. Many of the law course providers are private institutions, and external assistance with funding is limited. However, most of the colleges and universities offer bursaries and other schemes to assist talented candidates. You should check with your course provider to see if any options exist to assist with funding course fees.

There are also a number of important differences in the rules affecting European Union (EU) and non-EU students, including in relation to course fees and funding, and if you are from a non-EU country, you may be required to pay more than students from EU countries. You should look very carefully at how the immigration rules apply to you, and check with the course providers directly to ensure you have budgeted your fees and living expenses correctly.

Are your international qualifications recognised by the UK legal professional and regulatory bodies?

Earlier we mentioned the Solicitors Regulatory Authority (SRA) and Bar Standards Board (BSB) requirements to obtain a certificate of academic standing prior to studying the GDL, LPC or BPTC. It is essential that you check the current requirements, as set by the SRA or the BSB, in good time before you apply for any of the courses, to ensure that your home qualifications meet their eligibility criteria. You may be eligible to sign up to a course, but this in itself does not mean that your overseas academic qualifications will be recognised by the professional regulators. If they are not, then this will prevent you from going on to full qualification, even though you may have successfully completed one or some of the UK law courses.

Check the SRA and BSB websites for more information:

- www.sra.org.uk

- www.barstandardsboard.org.uk.

Are the qualifications you intend to gain in the UK recognised as valid back home?

The qualifications for solicitors and barristers administered by the SRA and BSB are valid for practice in England and Wales. While English legal qualifications have a high perceived status internationally, you must ensure that any qualifications you receive as a result of your studies in English law are formally recognised by the relevant institutions and regulatory bodies in your home country. The courses are costly and time-consuming: if you intend to make use of your English legal qualifications back home, then you need to know exactly how each qualification is recognised in your home country, well in advance of signing up to any courses, paying fees or making living or travel arrangements.

Language requirements

General language requirements for law

Excellent English is required at every stage of a career in law. Key elements of legal work include interpreting language, presenting and persuading others through verbal reasoning, understanding complex arguments, sifting through information, or researching cases, statutes and legal theory. Without a very solid grounding in English, it is not possible to perform well at the Academic or Vocational stages – and this is only the start. When it comes to working in legal practice, you will be stretched further, as your work gets more involved and you go deeper into the detail, with legal issues often appearing in complex contexts. In addition to understanding the law, and the facts behind any particular matter or issue you are working on, you will always be required to communicate clearly and concisely to colleagues and clients, in writing and in person.

Formal language requirements

Some course providers will only make offers to applicants whose first language is not English subject to proof that the applicant has an adequate command of English. This is usually done by sitting an International English Language Testing System (IELTS) test, where a score of 6.5 or above is usually required. When it comes to applying for training positions, you will often be expected to do a written test, as well as face-to-face interviews. Your skills in written and oral English will be tested, so it's essential that you have the required fluency before you start.

Life outside studying

Moving to a new country to study is a big decision. It is exciting and challenging, and you need to make sure you are properly prepared. If you have never lived in the UK before, do you know what to expect? Will you be able to adjust to the pace of life, perhaps in London, Manchester, or one of the other big cities? It may take time to adjust to life in the UK, and you need to know where to go for support when you need it, as well as building up a good network of friends and colleagues. Your college or university will provide as much help as they can, and you will not find it difficult to meet a lot of like-minded people. Many will also be from overseas and experiencing the same things as you, so they will be perfectly placed to accompany you on your journey through the various stages of legal qualification.

Qualified overseas lawyers who wish to practise in the UK

Qualified Lawyers Transfer Scheme (QLTS)

Lawyers qualified outside England and Wales, and some non-UK lawyers with English legal qualifications, may be entitled to have their qualifications recognised by the SRA and to become qualified solicitors in England and Wales. A test is involved, covering the key areas of property law, litigation, professional conduct and accounts, and principles of common law. Lawyers qualified overseas who wish to become solicitors in England should check with the SRA as to the current eligibility criteria and procedures in place, as requirements change from year to year.

For more information, see www.sra.org.uk/solicitors/qltt.page.

Registered European lawyers (RELs)

Lawyers qualified in European countries are permitted to practise as solicitors in other European countries, provided certain criteria are met. In order to practise in another European country, lawyers must be nationals of, and qualified in, one of the countries. They must use the professional title of the country's profession (in the original language), and must be registered with the professional regulatory body in the country. After three years' uninterrupted work in the host country, a lawyer qualified in another European country is eligible to be registered with the host country's legal profession, without sitting any exams or other assessments. REL registration is a complex process, and you should check with the SRA for more information.

A separate system exists for registered foreign lawyers (RFLs) wishing to become partners in law firms, or to take on other senior management roles. This system is available only to qualified lawyers at senior level, and is outside the scope of this book.

Conclusion

opefully you now have a good idea of what is involved in the most popular areas of legal work, and what to expect when working in them. We've covered how the profession works and what some of the roles entail, the various qualifications required and how to get them, as well as some of the key issues you might face when approaching the professional legal world outside your studies.

You will face challenges along the way, but with hard work, persistence and a good level of awareness of where you are headed and what is required to get there, there is nothing to stop you getting the job you want. Of course, some areas are harder to get into than others, but the vacancies are there, and they are filled by the most appropriate, best-skilled people – we've covered the basics here, so put this advice into practice, and get your name out there.

Good luck!

Glossary

ABS	Alternative Business Structures. Provisions of the Legal Services Act 2007 that came into force in October 2011 allow legal services to be provided in ways not previously permitted. ABS allows shareholder investment in law firms, and for non-legal organisations to offer legal services.
Academic Stage	The requirement for both solicitors and barristers to have completed either an undergraduate law degree, or postgraduate conversion. (*See* GDL.)
ADR	Alternative Dispute Resolution. A number of processes exist whereby parties to a dispute can seek resolution outside the expensive and public forum of the court system. ADR includes mediation, arbitration and expert determination.
Arbitration	A method of resolving legal disputes without going through the courts. The parties to the dispute elect an independent adjudicator (an 'arbitrator'), and agree to be bound by the arbitrator's decision. (*See also* ADR.)

Glossary

The Bar	The name given to the barristers' profession as a whole.
Bar Council	The approved regulator of the barristers' profession in England and Wales.
BPTC	Bar Professional Training Course. The current barristers' Vocational Stage qualification.
BSB	Bar Standards Board. Part of the Bar Council which takes on active regulatory functions of the barristers' profession.
Bundle	Files of documents, generally used in the context of litigation or court procedures, containing statements, evidence and correspondence between the parties. Junior lawyers are often called upon to help with putting bundles together ('bundling'), which can offer detailed insight into the elements and structure of a case.
BVC	Bar Vocational Course. The former barristers' Vocational Stage qualification, now replaced by the BPTC. (*See* BPTC.)
CAB	Central Applications Board. The www.lawcabs.ac.uk website is the only route applicants can apply for the full-time LPC and GDL courses.
Call	The number of years since a barrister was called to the Bar. Similar to post-qualification experience for solicitors. (*See* PQE.)
Called to the Bar	The process by which a barrister formally enters the profession. This is not the same as being a qualified practising barrister.
Chambers	A barrister's office, often shared with other barristers in a set. (*See* Set.)
CILEx	Chartered Institute of Legal Executives. A professional body and a provider of legal education.
Clerk	A barrister's administrative assistant, responsible for all aspects of booking, scheduling and fee recovery for the barrister.

Contentious	A legal matter that is subject to a dispute, regardless of the formal legal process being taken.
Conversion	A postgraduate course allowing graduates with a degree in a subject other than law to 'convert' to the equivalent of a law degree, and thereby satisfy the Academic Stage of training. This is either the Graduate Diploma in Law, or Common Professional Examination. (*See* GDL and CPE.)
Counsel	The formal word for a barrister, or the capacity of a barrister.
CPD	Continuing Professional Development. All solicitors and barristers are required to 'top up' their legal and professional knowledge after qualification.
CPE	Common Professional Examination. A qualification available to gain the Academic Stage qualification, now largely replaced by the Graduate Diploma in Law. (*See also* GDL.)
CPRs	Civil Procedure Rules. The CPRs and Practice Directions are the authoritative directory for court and litigation procedure.
Cross-examination	In court proceedings, the questioning of a witness by the opponent's legal representative, usually a barrister.
Examination-in-chief	In court proceedings, the questioning of a witness by their own legal representative. (*See also* Cross-examination.)
Fee	Charges made by solicitors and barristers to their clients, in return for their legal services.
Firm	A group of solicitors, usually working in partnership as a private practice. Many firms are now limited liability partnerships, rather than traditional partnerships. (*See* LLP.)
GDL	Graduate Diploma in Law. One of the conversion courses available to gain the Academic Stage qualification. (*See also* CPE.)

Glossary

Higher Rights of Audience	A qualification available to solicitors, allowing them to conduct advocacy in the higher courts (House of Lords, Court of Appeal, high court and Crown court).
Junior	A practising barrister who is not yet a QC. (*See* QC.)
Law firm	Usually a partnership of solicitors. (*See also* Firm.)
Law Society	The organisation representing the interests of solicitors in England and Wales. (*See also* SRA.)
Litigation	The formal legal process taken to resolve a dispute, in either civil or criminal law contexts. This may include court proceedings, or ADR. (*See* ADR.)
LLB	An undergraduate bachelor's degree in law. Comes from the Latin *Legum Baccalaureus*.
LLM	A postgraduate, master's degree in law. Comes from the Latin *Legum Magister*.
LLP	Limited Liability Partnership. Unlike traditional partnerships, where partners share unlimited liability for debts, negligence or misconduct, the LLP allows partners' liability to be limited, in a similar manner to limited companies. LLPs are still referred to as 'firms'. Many organisations, including law and accountancy firms, operate under this structure.
LPC	Legal Practice Course. The solicitors' Vocational Stage qualification.
Mediation	A form of ADR (*see* ADR) in which parties to a dispute elect an independent third party to assist them in negotiating a settlement to the dispute. The mediator does not act as an adjudicator, but as an intermediary.
NQ	For the first year after qualification, solicitors are referred to as 'newly qualifieds', or NQs.

PQE	Post-qualification experience. The number of years' experience that a solicitor has since qualification. For barristers. (*See* Call.)
PSC	Professional Skills Course. The final stage of the compulsory training – to ensure you are equipped with the necessary practical skills and knowledge to become a solicitor.
Pupil	A barrister in the final stage of training before obtaining a practising certificate.
Pupillage	The final stage of a barrister's training, after completing a law degree and the BPTC and being 'called to the Bar'.
QC	Queen's Counsel. The most senior lawyers in Commonwealth countries, selected from barristers or solicitors with Higher Rights of Audience. After appointment, QCs wear a silk gown in court appearances, hence the process of appointment being known as 'taking silk', and QCs being referred to as 'silks'.
Qualifying Law Degree	A law degree taken at undergraduate level, from an institution recognised by the Joint Academic Stage Board of solicitors and barristers.
REL	Registered European Lawyer.
RFL	Registered Foreign Lawyer.
Seat	A period of time, usually between four and six months, where a trainee solicitor will sit with a more senior supervisor in a particular department at a law firm.
Secondment	A placement undertaken by a trainee solicitor, pupil barrister or their qualified counterparts, where they join an organisation separate from their employer (perhaps a commercial client's offices, or government department), to work as a lawyer for that organisation. Secondments are

often used to offer experience to lawyers in training that their own firm, chambers or employer is unable to offer.

Set	A group of barristers, often sharing premises. (*See also* Chambers.)
Six	One of the two six-month stints that a pupil barrister will spend with a supervising junior.
SRA	Solicitors Regulation Authority. This is the independent regulatory arm of the Law Society of England and Wales, which is responsible for monitoring the training and qualification regulations of all solicitors in England and Wales.
Tenancy	The term used to describe a qualified, practising barrister's position within chambers.
Trainee	A future solicitor who has completed the Academic and Vocational stages, and who is in the process of completing their professional training, usually with a law firm.
Training Contract	The final stage required for qualification as a solicitor, usually completed with a law firm, and lasting two years.
Undertaking	A legally binding agreement or promise, often required to be taken by solicitors and trainees in the context of property transactions and other legal work.
Vocational Stage	The stage of training after the Academic Stage, satisfied by the BPTC and LPC, specific to barristers and solicitors respectively.
White Book	A leading publication from legal publishers Sweet & Maxwell containing the CPRs and Practice Directions, commentary and other resources for lawyers acting on contentious matters often in the county court, high court or Court of Appeal.

Endnotes

1. Law Society (2010) *Trends in the solicitors' profession: annual statistical report*, p.6.
2. *Ibid.*
3. ww2.prospects.ac.uk/p/types_of_job/barrister_salary.jsp
4. www.nus.org.uk/en/advice/money-and-funding/higher-education /average-costs-of-living-and-study
5. juniorlawyers.lawsociety.org.uk/node/140
6. www.sra.org.uk/solicitors/handbook/handbookprinciples/content.page

Useful resources

The Law Society: www.lawsociety.org.uk
Represents solicitors in England and Wales. Offers training and advice, and lobbies on behalf of the solicitors' profession at government level.

The Solicitors Regulation Authority (SRA): www.sra.org.uk
Regulates solicitors and is an independent regulatory body of the Law Society. The SRA sets standards and guidelines for the profession, monitors training and professional development, and issues practising certificates for qualified solicitors.

The General Council of the Bar, or Bar Council: www.barcouncil.org.uk
Regulates barristers in England and Wales, and operates its regulatory activities through a separate body, the Bar Standards Board.

For a full list of links to all resources and organisations mentioned in the book, visit www.charliephillips.info.

Index of advertisers